A HOLISTIC APPROACH TO YOUR CAREER

BLANCA DE LA ROSA

A HOLISTIC APPROACH TO YOUR CAREER

BLANCA DE LA ROSA

Copyright © August 2021

Certificate of Registration: TX 9-456-964

Blanca De La Rosa All rights reserved.

No part of this book may be used or reproduced by any means, graphic, electronic, or mechanical, including photocopying, recording, taping or by any information storage retrieval system without the written permission of the author except with brief quotations embodied in critical articles and reviews. Because of the dynamic nature of the Internet, any web addresses or links contained in this book may have changed since publication and may no longer be valid. The views expressed in this work are solely those of the author and do not necessarily reflect the views of the publisher, and the publisher hereby disclaims any responsibility for them. The author of this book does not dispense medical advice or prescribe the use of any technique as treatment for physical, emotional, or medical problems without the advice of a physician, either directly or indirectly. The intent of the author is only to offer general information to help you in your quest for emotional and spiritual well- being. In the event you use any of the information in this book for yourself, which is your constitutional right, the author and the publisher assume no responsibility for your actions.

ISBN: 978-1-83556-291-8   Paperback
ISBN: 978-1-83556-292-5   Hardback
ISBN: 978-1-83556-293-2   eBook

All rights reserved for all countries

The total or partial reproduction of this book, or the compilation in a computer system, or the transmission in any form or by any means, whether electronic, mechanical or by photocopy, by registration or by other means, neither the loan, rent or any other form of cession of the use of the copy without prior written permission of the copyright owners. "Any form of reproduction, distribution, public communication or transformation of this work can only be carried out with the authorization of its owners, except as otherwise provided by law"

CONTENTS

Introduction A Personal Perspective 7

PART I: A COMPREHENSIVE PERSPECTIVE

Chapter 01: A Balanced Career Approach.. 13
Chapter 02: Take the Initiative 19
Chapter 03: Continuous Learning 23
Chapter 04: Value of Communication Skills. 27
Chapter 05: Decisiveness 35
Chapter 06: Establish Yourself as a Leader.. 39
Chapter 07: We All Need Mentors. 43
Chapter 08: The Art of Networking.. 49
Chapter 09: Distinguish Yourself 55
Chapter 10: A More Confident You.. 59
Chapter 11: Business Acumen – Understanding the Big Picture.. ..63
Chapter 12: Quality Over Quantity.. 69

PART II: NAVIGATING THE WORK ENVIRONMENT

Chapter 13: Large Corporation or Small Company? . .. .75
Chapter 14: Managing a Bad Manager. 83
Chapter 15: Embrace Change.. 93
Chapter 16: Positive Disintegration 97
Chapter 17: Develop a Career Plan 111

PART III: WOMEN IN THE WORKPLACE

Chapter 18: Make Equality a Reality. 121
Chapter 19: The Female Leadership Conundrum 125
Chapter 20: Managing Personal Controversy 131
Chapter 21: Career, Family, or Both? 137

PART IV: EMPOWER YOURSELF FOR AN AMAZING CAREER

Chapter 22: Personal Empowerment – Why it Matters. 145
Chapter 23: Express Your Truth 149
Chapter 24: Trust Your Inner Guidance.. 153
Chapter 25: Defining Career Success 157
Bibliography 161
References 163
About the Author. 165

INTRODUCTION
A PERSONAL PERSPECTIVE

Over my forty-one-year professional career, I learned that there are certain attributes, skills, and action steps which are essential to career success and better positioning yourself for that next career move.

I started my corporate career in 1982 while still working on my undergraduate degree, and after six years in a small law firm. Nothing in my background had prepared me for a job in corporate America. Having grown up in a humble working-class environment, I entered the professional world with little to no knowledge of corporate etiquette and its unwritten rules. As I looked around our corporation, there were no role models, no one to emulate, no one to offer advice on the dos and don'ts of the corporate environment, so I had to do it my way. I had to learn things on my own by trial and error, making a lot of mistakes along the way. Some of these mistakes caused me some career moves, and others I overcame.

I spent the first eighteen years of my life in a predominantly Spanish-speaking environment within our slice of the Big Apple. We spoke Spanish at home, and most of the kids from my elementary and high school, the local businesses, and my circle of friends were of Hispanic descent. I had little to no exposure to other cultures. However, I did not understand the impact of this lack of diversity until I ventured into the working world as a legal secretary in Midtown Manhattan. Despite some similarities in my background with the other secretaries at the law firm, I seem to have missed a lot in the translation while growing up in New York City's Public Housing Development (The Projects). I had a lot of catching up to do.

The law firm took the girl out of the projects, but it was extremely difficult to take the projects out of the girl. Unlearning the behaviors of eighteen years does not happen overnight. Behavior modification is a long, continuous, and arduous journey that may or may not fully eradicate those learned behaviors. The behaviors, emotional reactions, and experiences I learned during the first eighteen years of my life became part of my personality. They are a subconscious part of who I am. It was the armor that protected me and helped me cope and navigate a volatile environment. These behaviors lay dormant in my subconscious as part of my personality, resurfacing when I feel threatened. There is a trace of that 'old me', that 'me' that you cannot see, hidden deep in my subconscious. That 'old me' resurfaces when some external event wakes it up and brings it forward. I've fallen back to familiar behavior when threatened, which, most times, has been an overreaction.

Many employees new to the professional world are uncertain about having to navigate their work environment. The informal education of navigating the corporate environment happens on the job by trial and error.

"A Holistic Approach to Your Career" is for those recently entering the corporate environment, providing guidance that they may not get in the classroom or at home. For those that need guidance and advice on how to advance their careers and move on after career failure or dealing with a bad, ineffective manager. Millions of employees are silently suffering through the abuse of a terrible manager or depressed about their inability to advance their careers.

My goal is to provide encouragement and impart the hard-earned wisdom gained throughout my forty-one-year career to the reader. Provide encouragement and guidance to those new to the professional environment and those who may want to continue to grow, expand, and be successful. The overarching message of this book is to inspire and motivate readers to forge ahead, no matter what trials and tribulations they encounter along the road to success.

This book is honest and pragmatic in its accounts of my professional experience and provides sound advice based on my reality, my personal experience. It features practical advice on how to manage conflict, tips on getting ahead, navigating the land mines and banana peels in the corporate world, and overcoming career failure.

In this book, I have detailed the items that I have found to be most critical when taking a holistic approach to your career. I do not mean the topics chosen to be all-inclusive or work for everyone. This selection may differ from one person to the other depending on their individual background and industry. I base this selection on my reality and experience. I encourage you to take and adhere to the items that resonate with you and leave the rest behind.

The overall tone is positive, uplifting, inspiring, and motivational, while realistic. It encourages readers to dare to dream and prepare and position themselves for that next promotion. The following pages contain information about personal career mistakes, guidance beneficial to anyone who dreams of building a successful career. I pair personal stories with strategies for overcoming adversity in the workplace.

You will discover how to take a holistic approach to your career, navigate the work environment, how to manage a bad manager, how to deal with career failure, how to develop a career road map, assess the journey of your career, and the importance of self-empowerment with uplifting and inspiring advice.

"A Holistic Approach to Your Career" offers a fresh approach and insight into climbing the corporate ladder, combining practical, common-sense advice with inner wisdom and spirituality, providing strategies to increase the chances of success in the workplace.

Who says you can't climb the corporate ladder—your boss, your co-workers, your parents' or siblings' negative programming?

How do you excel when the odds are overwhelmingly stacked against you every step of the way?

How does an immigrant, born in a small town in the Dominican Republic, and raised in New York City's public housing development, wind up in a corporation like Mobil Oil?

My son told me that a person from the South Bronx once asked him, "What does your mother do for a living?"

He responded, "She is a businesswoman at Mobil Oil Corporation."

The person responded, "People like us do not get jobs like that."

Well, they do, and I did, by empowering myself and creating an amazing career. I did so by not letting the naysayers get me down and by believing in myself and my abilities.

PART I

A COMPREHENSIVE PERSPECTIVE

CHAPTER 1
A BALANCED CAREER APPROACH

The first thing most people think about when they hear the word 'holistic' is a form of holistic medicine, which is the healing that considers the entire person (body, mind, spirit, and emotions) not just separate body parts. A holistic approach means thinking about something in its entirety. Understanding that the whole comprises interdependent parts that you must integrate for a successful outcome.

The holistic concept can also apply to your career, as upward mobility in any organization requires that you be well-rounded. The progression of your career and candidacy for job promotions require that you take a holistic approach. What does it mean to take a holistic approach to your career?

Taking a holistic approach to your career means taking a comprehensive perspective that considers every aspect of your work environment, which can lead to optimal career success and satisfaction. It requires that you consider everything from educational requirements to how you carry yourself at work. Ensuring that you strike a proper balance of the various aspects that make up the work environment.

More than a degree

Higher education will get you hired, but once you are on the job, you must prove and distinguish yourself from the competition. Demonstrating that you can contribute to the company's bottom line.

Succeeding in business requires a complete package that takes more than just a degree. Your experiences, skills, and abilities need to be varied and balanced; and determining which is more beneficial to a successful career, book smarts or street smarts, is exceptionally difficult, because it depends on the person and the circumstances.

You may know people who are book smart but do not have one ounce of common sense and are clueless about how to survive in the actual world. Others have the street smarts but do not know how to transfer or use those skills outside of their own environment. Those with a combination of education, job experience, and street smarts, with experience as the key ingredient, are the ones who are likely to be most successful.

Unfortunately, many corporations do not sufficiently value institutional knowledge and work experience when making career decisions. As a result, even if an employee has an excellent track record and has done exceptionally well in their job evaluations, when competing for a promotion or position with an MBA graduate, the credentials and luster of an MBA from a top business school will most likely win out.

A master's degree from any university is an excellent credential to have and, all things being equal, may give you the edge you need to prevail when competing for a job or promotion. So, depending on your industry and if you have the time, stamina, energy, and willingness, get that master's degree, even if it is part time, so that the next time education is the tiebreaker, you are the one with the edge to prevail.

Interpersonal skills

A successful career requires that you complement that formal education with informal education. You need to gain all the essential abilities and skills to deal with the growing demands of the personal and professional spheres. Besides your education and technical hands-on skills, you must develop and hone your interpersonal skills, also referred to as soft skills.

You need to understand and abide by those unwritten and unspoken rules and regulations that are part of your work environment and which are required in order to get ahead. The informal education of navigating your work environment happens on the job by trial and error.

You may have excelled in your educational pursuits and have excellent technological skills, knowledge, and other skills that specifically enable you to complete work-related tasks. But how good are your interpersonal skills? Are you self-confident? How are your communication, listening and networking skills?

Most of us focus and put a lot of emphasis on formal education and developing hard skills, but neglect to develop our interpersonal skills. To successfully use the technical knowledge and skill set you have gained, master those interpersonal skills that allow you to interact with others.

Interpersonal skills are personal attributes that allow you to relate to others. Applying these skills will help you build stronger relationships, work more productively, and maximize your career prospects. You cannot evaluate the value of interpersonal skills on any assessment metric, but they can be evaluated by others through your ability to maintain a balanced approach in your day-to-day handling of your job. Having a balanced approach to your work environment means that you are well-rounded and possess a perfect blend of technical and interpersonal skills.

While some people have better interpersonal skills than others, they are not innate, and anyone can learn the skill. You can enhance your interpersonal skills by first identifying which of those skills you are lacking and taking some training courses. You can ask your boss or a mentor to help you identify the skill gap.

You can develop soft skills in the same way you develop any other skill you practice. You can also seek opportunities to practice each individual skill in a low risk setting until you feel confident in your ability. For example, you don't have to be born a networker or a brilliant speaker. You can learn and build these skills throughout your career.

A productive and healthy work environment depends on its employees to have a blend of technical and interpersonal skills. The workplace is not a social club, but it is an interpersonal space that requires the building and fostering of relationships, perspectives and ideas exchanged, and conflicts resolved.

Interpersonal skills are on balance with professionalism. In its simplest terms, professionalism is the ability to strive to conduct yourself with responsibility, integrity, accountability, and excellence as you go about your day-to-day.

A holistic approach top ten

In the next ten chapters, I have detailed the top-ten items that I have found to be most critical when taking a holistic approach to your career. My top-ten items are not listed in order of importance, is not meant to be all-inclusive or work for everyone. This list may differ from one person to the other, depending on their individual background and industry. This selection is based on my reality and experience. I encourage you to take and adhere to the items that resonate with you and leave the rest behind.

1. **Take the initiative.** Always give people they need, not just what the job description's deliverables. Taking the initiative means going above and beyond your typical duties, taking charge of situations before others do.

2. **Continuous learning**. Stay on top of what is going on in your industry and understand how it can be affected by legislation, local events, or other world matters. Learning a new skill, technology, or process related to your industry—makes you smarter and increases your value as a person and an employee. Continuous learning is one of the best ways to further your career growth.

3. **Value of communication skills.** Your career survival and competitiveness can depend on your ability to communicate effectively. Develop both your verbal and written communication abilities. Get what you want by making your words count.

4. **Decision-making.** Decision-making is the process of choosing, solving problems utilizing your intuition or analyzing data or a combination of the two and it is at the heart of success. Decisiveness is an essential aspect of getting ahead. Decisive people are respected and tend to get promoted.

5. **Establish yourself as a leader.** You do not have to wait to be assigned a supervisory or managerial position to practice and develop your leadership style. Leadership skills are developed over time with practice and experience. If you aspire to have a formal

leadership position within your organization, you should start developing, refining, and defining your leadership style immediately. look for opportunities within your day-to-day activities to develop and exhibit your leadership skills.

6. **We all need mentors.** No matter the stage of your career, You will often need someone to help you navigate your work environment and point out the land mines. These should be people you know honestly believe in you and your abilities; and will help you navigate the challenges you may encounter in the workplace. Mentoring offers an opportunity to establish an informal one-on-one environment for coaching and feedback.

7. **The art of networking.** If you are serious about your career, learn how to network. Get out there and meet people. These people may have networks of their own that you can tap into to help you reach your career goals. Get to know people, so people can get to know you. Networking takes time and effort, but it is well worth the benefits you may derive.

8. **Distinguish yourself.** Identify your unique and transferable skills and strengths so you can define and refine your personal brand and enhance your marketability. Identify and master the skills required in your field. Which of your unique skills will you choose to distinguish yourself and stand out from the competition?

9. **A more confident you.** Self-confidence is a belief in oneself, in one's abilities, or one's judgment. It is freedom from doubt. Some people appear to be born with self-confidence, but most have to work at it. Self-confidence can be developed and nourished.

10. **Business acumen – understanding the big picture.** Business acumen is an ability that allows you to understand and cope with unique business situations. Business acumen is not any one particular skill, but a collection of competencies, knowledge, and awareness of multiple aspects of a particular business.

> *"Professional(ism) is not a label you give yourself,*
> *it's a description you hope others will apply to you."*
> **David Maister**

CHAPTER 2
TAKE THE INITIATIVE

"Your Success is your responsibility. Take the initiative, do the work, and persist to the end."
Lorii Meyers

It is important to know and understand what it means to take the initiative in order to use it properly to your advantage. It means being proactive and stepping up to handle a task, going above and beyond your typical duties and taking charge of situations before others do. It means being an innovator and thinking outside the box as you capitalize on and take advantage of the opportunities presented to you.

Taking the initiative puts you in the driver's seat and promotes a sense of personal power as you feel you are in control of the situation. It gives you a sense of achievement and accomplishment as you progress and get things done. It promotes an increased sense of self-confidence, a feeling of self-assurance, and self-awareness arising from the knowledge that you 'got this'.

Cultivating initiative

Now that you understand what it means to take the initiative and the benefits that you can derive, make taking the initiative a priority. If you are serious about progressing in your career, you must prepare yourself by keeping an eye out for opportunities presented to you. The ability to show initiative is one of the most crucial skills you can cultivate for a successful career. What can you do to cultivate initiative in your professional environment?

Go above and beyond your current assignment. Show that you are a go-getter and take the extra step when possible. Go above and beyond your current assignment by volunteering to take on additional responsibilities. However, before you volunteer, always make sure that you have the time and resources to complete the assignment in a timely, professional manner, never compromising the quality of your work.

Think beyond the surface. Think of the future benefits you can derive from helping others achieve their goals. Always give people what they need, not just the job's description of deliverables. If somebody needs to look good in front of their boss, then that's your assignment.

Display flexibility. Your flexibility shows your willingness to take on new tasks and challenges. Be flexible and willing to help your team where and when needed by taking on extra responsibilities and quickly adapting when priorities change.

Look for ways in which you can contribute to your team and your supervisor, even if it requires working some extra hours or working on projects to help someone else succeed.

Self-monitoring. Working well without the constant supervision of your boss will show your management your reliability and commitment and also show that you can take on a self-monitoring position which requires little to no management supervision.

Problem solver. Reporting a problem without a solution is not received well by management. You do not have to solve the problem alone. The ability to know who can help you reach a solution, and how they can do it, is half the battle. Thinking through a potential solution and volunteering your time to help resolve a problem or capitalize on an opportunity will assert your position as a reliable employee who takes the initiative and can handle a leadership role. Showcase your leadership skills by identifying and solving a particular problem in the work process.

Goals and objectives of your department. Keep abreast of what's going on in your company and be on the lookout for deficiencies. Once you have identified a deficiency, take the time to document your findings, propose a potential innovative solution, and volunteer your time to help close the gap or capitalize on the opportunity.

Make showing initiative a habit. Like any other skill, the more you work on showing initiative, the easier it becomes. The key is being resourceful and taking action or doing something before others do it or before you are told to do it. Be proactive, waiting to be told what or how to do something may be detrimental to your career.

Taking the initiative is a positive step that can offer some benefits and enhance your career prospects. It will give you a sense of self-control as you step up and take advantage of new opportunities and enhancing your confidence in yourself and your abilities. As you step-up and take charge, you will differentiate yourself from the competition and others will see you as a dependable leader, which may lead to a promotion as you showcase your talents. You can use taking the initiative as a tool to open doors to new opportunities as it sets you apart and helps you stand out from your colleagues.

Your management may not always present or offer opportunities to showcase your talent and there will be times when you have to take matters into your own hands by identifying opportunities to stand-out. This may be the only way to prove that you can contribute to the bottom line of the organization and add value while simultaneously enhancing and developing new skills.

Performing a task that is reserved for those at a much higher level than your current assignment is an excellent way to show your abilities, skills, strengths, leadership skills, and your desire to have a bigger role within the organization.

Volunteering and helping my group worked exceptionally well for me. Our group was understaffed, and the analysts did not have sufficient time to run all the required economics and spreadsheets. I took full advantage of this deficiency by volunteering to help and it allowed me to learn the business.

My efforts did not go unnoticed by my department manager. He was so impressed by my ability to perform duties assigned to analysts at a much higher level that he lobbied to move me out of the secretarial job. He advocated that the corporation was not capitalizing on my skills and talents by keeping me in a secretarial position.

After two years, with a lot of hard work, determination, and a powerful mentor, I received a two-level promotion into the administration group as a contract documentation specialist.

I had accomplished what many said was impossible: a promotion out of the secretarial realm into an administrative staff position before the completion of my formal education. My informal education and hard work were working for me. A twogroup promotion from a secretarial position into the administration group was rare, and a significant milestone for me.

> *"If you're going to be truly successful, then set yourself apart from everyone else. Go beyond the limits of what classifies the average person and be exceptional."*
> **Beyond the Quote Motivational Business Quotes**

CHAPTER 3

CONTINUOUS LEARNING

"Learning is a weightless treasure you can always carry easily."
Chinese Proverb, A Collection of Wisdom

Continuous learning is ongoing self-directed learning, formal or informal education, keeping up with technology and changes in your industry.

It can come in many forms, from formal course taking to casual social learning. Learning a new skill, technology, or process related to your industry—whether it is on-the-job training or class at your community college or business school, executive management program, or some other organization that provides training for professionals—makes you smarter and increases your value as a person and an employee.

There are many options to choose from when pursuing an education. You do not have to take time out of your busy schedule to travel to a university. You can take online classes, which are extremely convenient for full-time employees, as they are readily accessible anytime and anyplace.

My personal favorites were the on-the-job training courses offered by our company. I took advantage of and exhausted all training opportunities the company provided. On-the-job training is usually free for the employee and conducted during your workday. The training offered by your company is usually information or a skill set that your company perceives to be valuable to the company's viability. Many corporations not only welcome but encourage employees to take full advantage of these opportunities.

These training courses can range from technical to computer software skills. The main objective is to make sure you have the skill set required to get that next promotion. Check out your company's training courses. Invest the time, clear your schedule, and make time to take a training course or two. This is one of the best ways to increase your net worth within your organization.

Why it matters

Staying competitive means that you need to be innovative, adaptive, and ever-changing. To innovate, to try a new process, or to do something new requires continuous learning. Employees should challenge themselves in order to obtain new knowledge, ideas, and skills which can expand their horizons and bring new ideas and innovation to the workplace. Learning needs to be on a flexible, on-demand and on a continual basis in order to contribute this kind of cutting-edge performance.

Continuous learning will help in the development of your career, as you will stay marketable and will be prepared for that next promotion, or career change. Learning a new skill and acquiring knowledge will give you a new point of view and perspective on things, can enhance a work process, and will keep you abreast of new technology.

This commitment to continuous learning and learning the business from the ground up was the fundamental building block of my career. Early in my career, I committed to enhancing my formal education with informal education because I believed that this combination was going to be my ticket to a successful career with the company. I read all the periodicals I could get my hands on so I could learn how the energy industry worked, how our company fit into the industry, and how my current position fit into the bigger picture.

Develop a learning plan

A learning plan is a description of how you intend to achieve your desired learning. Your plan can range from a simple list of items to a structured formal and orderly plan. There is no one perfect, standard format for a learning plan. Your plan should suit your specific personal circumstances and needs. You can make it a living document and adjust it as you go along.

You can start developing your plan with the following:

- Identify specific, achievable goals – What do you want to accomplish?
- Identify skill gaps – Does your goal require a specific skill set?
- Determine which training style will work best for you – Does your goal require job training or university degree?
- Identify learning venue and availability – What is available and affordable for you? Does your company offer training? Can you take online classes? Does your particular skill set require hands-on in person participation?
- Once you have identified your goals, required skills, required training and venue, select the activities best suited to help you reach your goals, weigh all of your options and develop your plan.
- Assess your plan frequently, evaluate, and reflect. Frequent assessments will help you stay on track with your professional developmental goals.

Corporate environment. If you find yourself in a corporate environment, review your individual learning plan with your manager for approval and to gather feedback on whether it is workable. Once your manager gives you the go-ahead, get started and make adjustments along the way. Review your progress at certain intervals to ensure that your learning is on track with your career goals and celebrate your successes.

Changing jobs. If you are preparing for a new position within or outside of your company, your individual learning plan should include the skills required to best position yourself for the new assignment.

Also, ensure that your plan aligns with the timing requirements of the new company.

Creating a learning plan will provide structure and help support your career and personal development goals so you can focus on that next career move.

Regardless of which venue you choose, continuous learning is one of the best ways to further your career growth. No matter the stage of your career, never stop learning. There is always a need to grow your knowledge base, improve, or learn a new skill. Technology and software are constantly being updated, and you must always strive to stay on top of the latest software required by your industry.

Continuous learning keeps you engaged and challenged in your job and career. Being well-rounded and well-read will take you far, as you will be well-versed in various topics. Stay on top of what is going on in your industry and understand the impact of legislation, local events, or other world matters.

Reading can open up your creative mind to new ideas and manner of thinking. It will expand your vocabulary and knowledge and may trigger an innovative idea to improve a work process. Commit to continuous, informal and formal learning, growing as a person, and learning from your mistakes.

> *"Education is the passport to the future,*
> *for tomorrow belongs to those who prepare for it today."*
> **Malcolm X**

CHAPTER 4

VALUE OF COMMUNICATION SKILLS

*"Communication, the human connection,
is the key to personal and career success."*
Paul J. Meyer

Your career survival and competitiveness can depend on your ability to communicate effectively. Everyone from the CEO to the lowest level employee must be able to inform, persuade, and motivate diverse groups. The higher you move up in the organization, the more important it will become that you can address senior management, present ideas, and represent your company or yourself at industry functions.

What is communication? The definition of communication is "the imparting or interchange of thoughts, opinions, or information by speech, writing, or signs, successfully conveying or sharing of ideas and feeling."

There are three primary forms of communications: verbal, non-verbal, and written. Communication is not just about what comes out of our mouths. In fact, what we don't say, our body language, voice intonation and use of silence often send a louder message to other people than the words that come out of our mouths.

Verbal communication

There are two aspects of speech, *'what you say'* is verbal and *'how you say it'*, your tone, pitch, and volume are paraverbal. We are often oblivious to how we come across in conversation, not focusing on how we say things.

Did you know that the tone of your voice can inject emotions into messages? Messages can be upbeat or depressing depending on the tone of your voice. If you change how, you pronounce words by stressing or emphasizing certain syllables can change its meaning. The pace of your speech or the deliberate pauses in phrases can change the meaning of your message and convey a sense of urgency, sympathy, or negligence. The volume of your voice is also important, as being too loud or too soft can convey different messages. A voice that is too soft can convey nervousness or weakness, while we can perceive a loud voice as angry or aggressive. Your pronunciation and enunciation of words can influence whether your message is interpreted correctly.

Ineffective verbal communication leads to confusion, poor decisions, and can have an adverse impact on your career progression. One way to perfect your verbal communication skills is to hone your listening skill. Communication goes both ways, and you have to stop speaking long enough to listen to the perspective of others. *"Hearing is through the ears, but listening is through the mind." – Anonymous.* Hearing is the sense that helps you receive sound waves and noise through the ears. Listening is the ability to receive and interpret the message conveyed by someone else during conversation. Good listening skills will help you learn and properly respond to the circumstances presented.

Another way to improve your verbal communication skills is to take a speaking course, preferably one that videotapes your progress, so that you can learn how to present with confidence and conviction. For example, Toastmasters helps people overcome the fear of public speaking and is especially suitable for people that are shy or lack confidence. A formal course can help you gain confidence in presenting your material, overcome nervousness and inhibitions, and help you plan your thoughts when under pressure.

Feeling some nervousness and apprehension before giving a speech is natural and can be beneficial, as it keeps you alert, focused, and aware of your surroundings and audience. However, too much nervousness can be detrimental and cause you to draw a blank on portions of the message you intend to deliver. If you falter, do not apologize as this will only draw attention to your mistake. Chances are no one noticed. Most people are not active listeners and most likely will not remember 100% of what they heard. Also, keep in mind that your audience does not want you to fail; they have invested their time so you can inform, stimulate, and entertain them with your speech.

When I have to deliver a speech, regardless of the length, I first identify my audience and the key message I want to deliver. I make sure that I am well-versed in the material I'm about to deliver by writing it down, as this helps me to remember all the major points. I practice out loud or rehearse the speech in my mind. Practicing helps me with the flow and ensures that I stay within the time limit. If possible, I like to get a feel for the room and equipment. For example, I have discovered that I do not feel comfortable with a handheld microphone; I prefer a lavaliere or lectern with a microphone attached. These little preferences can make an enormous difference in your comfort and ease while delivering your message. Discover your preferences as soon as you can. Developing your speaking style and preferences will be a priceless skill to possess as you progress your career.

Addressing an audience, whether it is your peers, management, or delivering a speech in public, takes practice. The more you practice, the faster you will identify your strengths and weaknesses and develop a style that works for you early in your career. The more you practice with internal presentations or delivering speeches to external audiences, the faster you can refine your speaking style. Practice builds experience and confidence, which are the keys to effective speaking; so, accept as many speaking engagements as you can.

Nonverbal communication – body language

Body language is non-verbal communication involving gestures, postures, and physiologic signs, which act as cues for other people. For example, putting your hands on your hips, folding your arms across your chest, waving your arms, or your posture can send a definitive message. It is the process of communication through sending and receiving wordless messages that are the most powerful form of communication. Nonverbal communication cues others about what is in your mind, even more so than your voice or words.

Understanding body language will give you insight into the thoughts and feelings of those around you. Body language is a nonconscious form of communication people betray themselves with because:

- it honestly conveys your true feelings
- it creates self-awareness as understanding body language helps you identify your own actions that may hinder your success
- it helps you understand feelings and motive such as aggression, submission, deception which you can use as cues to your communication
- it enhances listening and communication skills as you learn to detect inconsistencies between the spoken word and the person's body language

You cannot underestimate the importance of unspoken communication, as it makes up over half of what we tell others and they tell us. It improves your negotiating, management, and interpersonal skills as you correctly interpret body language and important signals others are emitting.

We've all heard that 'actions speak louder than words' meaning that how we perceive each other is based on more than what we say to each other. For example, people can negotiate, have cordial, casual conversation and not even like each other. However, their body language or other actions can make a stronger impression than their words. A person can dismiss you with a roll of their eyes or the wave of a hand without saying one word. Whether we want to or not, our body language makes a lasting impression on others.

Written communication

While the value of outstanding verbal communication skills cannot be diminished, you cannot minimize or ignore the value of written communication skills, as they are equally essential for effective communication. Written communication can be via text messages, emails, letters, a simple note, articles, or any other form of writing.

Writing well is a skill that you can learn, develop, and nourish. However, this process takes time, patience, practice, and focus. Give yourself sufficient time to think through and develop your topic, whether you are writing internal memos, corresponding with clients, or writing a technical position paper.

Getting started is the hardest part,

- Start at the beginning, middle, or end of your message. Start putting thoughts on paper, capturing whatever comes to your mind on the topic without concerning yourself about typos, verb tenses, or flow.
- When you have run out of thoughts, go to the beginning and read what you have written and edit, delete, and expand on ideas. Do this until you have fully developed your thoughts.
- Go back and 'unclutter' your document, removing redundancies, qualifiers, or other words and thoughts that do not add value or support your message.
- As a last step, make sure you carefully proofread your document. Depending on the importance of your document, have someone else read it. A fresh pair of eyes may pick up things you've missed.
- If you have the luxury of time, put the document away for a day or so and then review with a fresh mind.

In today's environment, with most people opting to write e-mails, text messages, or instant messages, it is vital to get your point across in a few lines. So, your communication must be crisp, clear, concise, and effective. Many people are lazy about reading and may ignore your message if it is too long or drawn out.

The better your writing skills are, the better the impression you will make. You can never take the quality of a written document for granted, because it takes on a life of its own after you send it. You never know how someone may use it or how far a favorable impression might take you. Take the time to identify your targeted audience and the message you want to convey in a concise and professional manner.

One caution on written communication is to beware of the poison-pen syndrome. Today, many people are reluctant to pick up the phone or walk down the hall. Most of our communication is in writing. We must be cautious of how we respond and what we commit to writing.

Do not respond to an e-mail when you are still angry and reacting to someone else's hostility. This type of response on your part can be lethal for your career. It may feel good to get it off of your chest, but I guarantee you will regret writing it when your own words come back to haunt you. Leaving written evidence that puts you in an unfavorable light can wreak irreparable damage to your career.

Sending angry or derisive memos, e-mails, or text messages might make you feel better for the moment, but they can seriously damage your credibility and career. Your boss or human resources department may not be privy to the entire story when they are viewing your derogatory message and may use your own words against you.

Instead, use the poison pen to write your initial draft and get it off your chest, but do not send it. Sleep on it, and then come back to it when you have cooled off. It will amaze you at how your perspective can change overnight. Do yourself and your career a favor: stop, think, and reflect before you write and send a message.

Finally, just like any other skill, you must practice, practice, and then practice some more. The more you do it, the easier it gets, and the benefits you will derive from excellent communication skills are priceless.

Communication skills are one of the most valuable skills you need to develop for a successful career. Get what you want by making your words count. Excellent verbal communication skills are priceless as you negotiate on your own behalf or when representing your company. An effective communicator has the power of persuasion and can influence and guide decision-makers. It will give you the ability to exchange thoughts effectively and clearly convey ideas when trying to reach a consensus or a mutually acceptable solution.

Effective communication is a fundamental skill that all leaders or aspiring leaders should possess. Leaders are respon-sible for presenting the company's views on a public issue or its own mission, vision, and values. Leaders must also be able to communicate strategy, guidance, and direction to their employees. Ineffective communication leads to confusion, poor decisions, and a lack of leadership. What good is it to be a master in your field if you cannot adequately convey your knowledge to others?

Make it a priority to develop your communication skills early in your career, as excellent communication skills are necessary in all walks of life.

> *"You can have brilliant ideas, but if you can't get them across,*
> *Your ideas won't get you anywhere."*
> **Lee Iacocca**

CHAPTER 5

DECISIVENESS

"Indecision is the greatest thief of opportunity."
Jim Rohn

Decision-making is one of the key ingredients for a successful career. However, just making a decision isn't sufficient, as bad or hasty decisions can cost you your career. The ability to make quick decisions characterizes decisiveness; but it does not mean recklessness or impulsiveness.

Decisions need to be made carefully and mindfully, not on emotions or external pressure. Before you decide, you need to weigh and balance your options, so that you ultimately decide based on the best information available to you. Decisiveness combines the ability to put things into perspective, weigh the options, assess all relevant information, and accept any consequences.

Decisiveness is an essential aspect of getting ahead. Management respects and promotes decisive employees. They stay calm under pressure, take charge during a crisis and usually have a plan which they execute with purpose and direction. A decisive employee will take effective and considered action quickly, especially when under pressure. They take responsibility for the consequences of their decision and can adapt when they make mistakes.

The indecisive person is excruciatingly and painfully slow to decide. As a result, they make little to no progress in their careers. They get stuck, petrified by the thought of having to decide. In the meantime, opportunities pass them by, and they never seem to move toward their goals. The thought that making one decision might close the door to an alternative opportunity petrifies them.

Some crucial decisions can be frightening, but sometimes, not deciding can cause you to lose a unique opportunity that may not be available at a later time. Strive to seize the opportunity when presented to you.

Decision-making techniques

Decision-making and solving problems involve choosing between various potential solutions to a situation through your intuition or using some process to evaluate and analyze the facts. Sometimes, you will need to use a combination of the two.

From time to time, we have all struggled with making a certain decision. However, for some people it is a bit more complicated, because they like to please everyone. They don't want to make waves or let anyone down, which leads to indecision for fear of hurting someone's feelings. While others tend to over-analyze things and become paralyzed by their own analysis.

Think about past decisions. Is this situation similar to a past decision? In that case, what did you learn from that last decision? It's often been said that those who don't understand history are doomed to repeat it. Sometimes we make the same poor decisions repeatedly.

You don't always have the luxury of time to sit down and analyze a situation, and it is, therefore, harder to make the right choice under pressure. In those situations, go with your intuition, your gut feelings. Several scientific studies have shown that a correct gut feeling can hit us before our brains can even rationally process what is going on. Think of the many times you ignored your gut feelings just to have them confirmed at a later time.

While listening to your gut seems straightforward, most people ignore these feelings. Unfortunately, intuition doesn't always seem rational, and you may think you are overreacting or making too much of something because it rarely spells things out, giving instructions you can clearly understand.

We are constantly being bombarded with intuitive messages in different forms. Sometimes it's a gut feeling when you know that something is not right or that something is about to happen, but you do not have any evidence to substantiate or define the feeling. Sometimes it can be an overwhelming feeling that you should be elsewhere, doing something or avoiding a certain place or thing. Or it can be a fight-or-flight response that causes those little hairs on the back of your neck to stand up, to warn you that something bad is about to happen.

In all cases, the messages aren't always as clear as we would like them to be or as easy to understand, which is probably why many people do not follow their intuition. Even though the messages aren't always clear, they can sometimes be repetitive, and that is when you need to pay attention to your intuition. It is worth examining your gut feeling if you have a powerful feeling against a particular decision to see if you can figure out whether the feeling justifies further action.

More complicated decisions require a more formal, structured approach, usually involving both intuition and analyzing the facts and figures involved with each decision.

Learning to empower yourself by taking the driver's seat in the decision-making process will go a long way. Weigh the pros and cons of each option and consider the absolute worst thing that could happen and whether you could live with that worst-case scenario. If possible, 'try on' your decision, wear it for a day, and see how it feels. Then let those feelings either guide you toward that option or steer you away.

Finally, if you still can't decide, and everything being equal with your options, toss a coin. Pay attention to your feelings when the coin is in the air. Are you secretly hoping for a specific outcome? Are you disappointed or elated by the outcome of the toss? Your feelings can be an indicator of which option you should choose.

There are many websites that provide help and guidance for making efficient and effective decisions. Surf the web or your bookstore and browse until you find a book, article, or program that resonates with you and your gut feelings.

Decisions are at the heart of success, and there are critical moments when they can be difficult, perplexing, and nerve-wracking. When faced with hard choices, evaluate, investigate, and make an informed decision.

> *"One of the most important things I have learned…is that life is all about choice. On every journey you take, you face choices. At every fork in the road, you make a choice. And it is those decisions that shape our lives."*
> **Mike DeWine**

CHAPTER 6

ESTABLISH YOURSELF AS A LEADER

"A good leader inspires people to have confidence in the leader; a great leader inspires people to have confidence in themselves."
Eleanor Roosevelt

Leadership is not defined by your job title, and it is certainly not limited to your boss or senior management. You do not have to wait to be assigned a supervisory position to practice and develop your leadership style. Leadership skills are developed over time with practice and experience. The development of leadership skills happens over time with practice and experience.

If you aspire to have a formal leadership position within your organization, start developing, refining, and defining your leadership style immediately. There are many leadership styles and combination of styles. I have selected the five I thought would be most relevant.

Transactional. The transactional leadership approach depends on a system of rewards and punishments and emphasizes getting things done 'by the book' staying within the boundaries and rules of the organization. The transactional style abounds in the bureaucratic environment of large organizations.

Transformational. The transformational approach focuses on reaching the goals of the team and effecting change by serving as a role model, inspiring, motivating, mentoring, and nurturing in a participative and collaborative environment.

Autocratic. The autocratic leader subscribes to the 'my way or the highway' philosophy. Believing that they have the autonomous power to decide on behalf of their teammates, without consulting them.

Situational. Versatile leaders base their leadership style on the situation, issue, or particular environment tailoring their approach to the particular circumstances.

Visionary. Visionary leaders recognize that the processes, steps, and methods of their leadership style involves working through and with people. Visionary leaders inspire change and drive progress by earning trust for new ideas.

Honing your leadership skills

If you are currently in an individual contributor position, meaning that you do not have a staff reporting to you, look for opportunities within your day-to-day activities to develop and exhibit your leadership skills. There are many ways in which you can develop and hone your leadership skills without a formal title.

Dependable problem solver. Establish yourself as a leader by demonstrating you are a dependable problem-solver, a great resource, and always a team player who will offer solutions to problems and invest the required time and effort to ensure that things get done. For example, if you identify a problem within your working environment, go to your boss and advise him of the issue, provide a solution to the problem.

Lead a work team. Seize any opportunity to lead a work team as it is the perfect venue for showcasing and honing your leadership skills. If an initiative requires leading a team, listen to your team members and colleagues. Lead brainstorming sessions with your team to ensure that everyone can voice their thoughts. These sessions may generate an innovative idea that will make you look like a hero, and your team members will appreciate your inclusive behavior, being heard, and believe in your ability to lead. As the team leader, the outcome of the initiative is your responsibility. If things don't work out, you will deliver the message to your management. If things work out well, you will get the credit. I encourage you to make sure that you recognize and give credit to the rest of the team. After all, you did not accomplish the results by yourself; it was a team effort.

Social groups and events. Are there any social or employee resource groups in your work environment? If so, think about volunteering to head an internal event or running for office. This is an excellent opportunity to develop your leadership skills in a safe, low risk setting and environment. For example, I served as vice president and then president of our Latino organization, representing our Latino employees within the company. I also represented our company at many external events hosted by our organization's foundation. This option will help you develop and refine your leadership, communication, and networking skills as you host both internal and external events.

Find your voice. Develop and perfect your speaking style by accepting as many speaking engagements as you can. Leaders or aspiring leaders should possess the ability to speak in public and address their employees. As a leader, you will communicate strategy, guidance, and direction to your employees or represent your company at industry functions.

Mentor someone. Volunteer to mentor another employee that can benefit from your experience. Serving as a mentor is an excellent way to improve your leadership skills and can also be extremely rewarding. Mentoring can be mutually beneficial, as you can bring out the best in others and help them reach their highest potential while increasing your effectiveness as a leader. My most rewarding role was serving as a mentor to the junior employees in our company, guiding them through the corporate maze in the early years of their careers.

Get a mentor. Have someone mentor you. A mentor can coach you on actions you can take to help you develop your leadership skills and how to be an effective supervisor.

Create a Leadership mission statement. What type of leader are you determined to be? Write a statement that defines who you will become. If you are having trouble, think of a leader you admire, list the qualities you would like to emulate and why then use that as a starting point.

Educate yourself on leadership. There are many websites and books on leadership. Surf the web or go to your local bookstore and browse until you find a book or program that meets your needs and start developing your leadership style.

It is never too early to hone your leadership skills. When developing your leadership style, remember that an effective leader inspires and influences others by example, helping others within a positive environment to reach their fullest potential.

Leadership matters

Leadership matters because rarely do things come to success without solid leadership. When everything is going well, it is leadership that keeps people from taking their eye off the ball. When things go awry, it is leadership that sets the new course and provides hope and confidence.

People look to leaders to guide, lead, motivate, and support them. In fact, many employees look up to and emulate great leaders within their organizations. Leaders get to set the tone and tenor of their environment.

Leaders possess attributes that distinguish them from their peers, that their co-workers can look up to, and that management can depend on. Strive to emulate some of the personal qualities possessed by all prominent leaders: *honesty, integrity, commitment to high standards, self-confidence, flexibility, and interpersonal skills.*

Some people are born natural leaders, while others have to work on it. The good news is that you can nurture and develop your leadership skills. Leadership skills are invaluable if you're running your own business or looking to start one.

Those with strong leadership skills can inspire others and lead teams to success. Don't be shy about demonstrating your leadership potential by demonstrating how you have positively influenced others or taken a project to success.

> *"To be a leader is not to have a huge position. To be a leader is to see your job as the chance to inspire the world, no matter what your job is."*
> **Robin Sharma**

CHAPTER 7

WE ALL NEED MENTORS

*"People seldom improve when they have
no other model but themselves to copy."*
Oliver Goldsmith

No matter the stage of your career, a little mentoring along the way is always a smart idea. You will often need someone to help you navigate your work environment and point out the land mines. These should be people you know honestly believe in you and your abilities; and will help you navigate some of the challenges you may encounter in the workplace.

What is a mentor and a mentee?

A mentor is an experienced personal guide, trustworthy advisor, personal champion, constructive critic, and motivator that helps develop the career of a mentee. Someone who can offer wisdom and encouragement to a mentee, providing unique insights into situations that the mentee may not have otherwise considered. The mentor teaches the mentee how to navigate the work environment and inspires the mentee to become the best version of themselves. A mentor's primary goal is to help the mentee succeed.

The mentee, also called the protégé, is the student who needs the expertise and guidance of the mentor's knowledge and experience. The mentee will take action, practice, and show how the guidance has helped in the development of their career.

What is a mentoring relationship?

A mentoring relationship is a multi-layered experience in which both people benefit. The mentor guides the mentee through their journey of discovery. The mentor benefits as the relationship helps the mentor cultivate their leadership and communication skills. Mentoring is a partnership between two individuals in which both the mentor and the mentee derive benefits.

Do not limit yourself to just one mentor or one gender, as it is unlikely that one mentor will fulfill all of your developmental needs. Try to find a successful male and female to mentor you, as there will be times when you will need advice from a male, and other times it will be a female. These should be people you know believe in you and your abilities. People that will help you navigate the challenges you may encounter in the corporate environment.

You can also choose to have a mentor within your company (internal mentor) and someone within your same industry (external mentor). The internal mentor can help with current issues within your workplace, while the external mentor can help with broader career and professional moves within your industry. The mentoring relationship motivates the mentee to follow through on the mentor's guidance and succeed in their career.

At times, you can encounter some challenges with the mentoring relationship, such as pairing mentor and mentee, the feedback from mentor to mentee can be perceived as too negative, the logistics of coordinating meeting times, and there can also be a potential personality clash.

The mentoring relationship should be the catalyst that stimulates the progression of the mentee's career. The relationship should be dynamic and collaborative, requiring the participation of both the mentor and mentee in a synergistic relationship.

The mentoring relationship life-cycle

There are four primary stages to mentoring relationships: initiation; definition and agreement of the structure of the relationship; redefinition of relationship; and termination of the relationship.

Initiation. During the initiation stage, you meet your mentor and establish a baseline of skills. Both the mentor and mentee will clarify their needs, state a clear vision, establish goals, and establish what both are looking for in the mentoring relationship.

Definition of relationship. After you have met your mentor, you will define and agree on the structure of the relationship. The mentor and mentee decide on the mentee's goals, including the timeline for the initial relationship and the logistics of mentoring sessions.

Redefinition. After a defined period, it is wise for the mentor and mentee to redefine their roles. As the mentee grows professionally, the two may become friends, or more like peers. In this phase of the mentoring relationship, the mentee has grown both professionally and personally and may want to redefine the roles.

Termination of relationship. The time will come for the mentoring relationship to end. Either the mentor or the mentee can initiate the termination process or it could be a mutual decision if both recognize that the relationship is not working. The relationship can end for many reasons: the company transfers one or the other to another location or moves away for personal reasons; the skills match is not beneficial to the mentee; there could be a personality clash, and the mentor and mentee cannot bond; the relationship is not fulfilling, as one or the other does not take their responsibilities seriously and cannot meet their commitments; the mentee has reached their goals, and the mentor has passed on the required knowledge; priorities and availabilities may have changed. Regardless of the reason, during this phase, open and honest communication will help both the mentor and mentee transition to better suited mentoring relationship.

Benefits of mentoring program

Mentoring can help the mentee in both their personal and professional development, as it is an excellent way to get the lay of the land and receive good third-party advice on skills development and interpersonal relationships. It offers the mentee an opportunity to establish an informal one-on-one environment for sharing and leveraging experiences, coaching and feedback from someone they can trust to use as a sounding board during challenging times. The mentoring relationship offers the mentee the opportunity to learn from someone else's mistakes and successes.

Serving as a mentor is an excellent way to improve your leadership skills and can also be rewarding as you see the mentee, develop and your role in shaping a new generation of professionals. The mentor can also learn from the mentee, as the younger generation is well versed in new technology. The mentee also brings a fresh perspective with new ideas on how to enhance a work process.

To be involved in a mentoring relationship is a privilege for both participants, and as a result, it is important to be gracious and thoughtful towards each other.

Formal and informal mentoring programs

There are many mentoring relationships available. However, all of those relationships fall under one of two buckets, formal and informal. If your company offers a mentoring program, you can participate in a structured program. If not, you can develop an informal relationship with a colleague, or you can identify a senior manager or senior employee that you believe can help you achieve your goals.

Formal program. A structured, formal mentoring program partners mentors and mentees with the goal of matching less experienced workers with seasoned employees for career development, guidance, and support. This structure allows an organization to offer its employees a valuable tool that can assist the mentor by keeping the protégé on track and providing the skills they need to reach their personal career goals.

A structured program is ideal for the person who is shy. It is for the person who finds approaching someone they do not know uncomfortable. This program eliminates the need for the protégé to make the first move.

If you choose a formal mentoring program, try to commit to the program for at least one hour per month for one full year. The relationship should not be prescriptive. You should tailor the time to your specific needs. But, if the relationship is not working, or the chemistry is just not there, do not be shy about expressing your feelings. After all, the relationship should be about your self-development and benefit, and you have to feel comfortable with your mentor. Likewise, your mentor has to feel that he or she has the skills, abilities, and time to help you.

Informal program. An informal mentoring relationship can develop naturally with a boss or colleague, takes place in every organization and is highly effective. The knowledge transfer that results from an informal relationship is extremely beneficial for both the mentor and protégé.

Identifying someone that you respect or someone that may have pursued a career path that you may have an interest in exploring is another method for establishing an informal mentoring relationship. Most people will readily agree when asked to be a mentor and if they have the time and ability will do so. Once you have identified a potential mentor, schedule a meeting or lunch to discuss a potential mentoring relationship. During this conversation, establish the following:

- Do not assume that the person can serve as a mentor. Ask the person if they have the time and ability to help you achieve your goals. If the person does not have the time, ask if they feel comfortable recommending someone else to coach and counsel you.
- Your career goals and how you believe this mentoring relationship will help you achieve your goals.
- Your expectation of the mentoring relationship.
- Why you chose him/her as a mentor. Give specific feedback on their strengths and characteristics, which led you to believe they could help you reach your career goals.
- Establish the timing and frequency of meetings.

For mentoring to work best, the mentor and mentee should establish a completely open relationship and a haven to share experiences and talk openly about strengths and weakness. Topics can include corporate values, reward and recognition, setting goals, your upcoming performance review, or specific projects. There are no limits to what you can discuss.

Long-term mentoring relationship

The ideal mentoring relationship develops into a longterm professional and personal relationship. Mentoring is most powerful and impactful when it occurs over a long period, as the mentor and mentee build rapport and trust over the years. Over the mentoring relationship, deep bonding and trust occur. Long-term mentoring can be very influential in supporting the mentee's growth in both their personal and professional endeavors and develops into an extended family relationship.

I have served as a mentor for many young professionals over the years. In a handful of cases, they have developed into long-term relationships. Some of these youngsters have become part of my extended family as I've seen them develop into successful professionals, get married, and have children of their own. I view each of them as I do my own children.

Having a mentor, formal or informal, is like having access to a personal trainer. It gives you access to someone who can help you build exceptional skills. This personal career trainer is at your disposal, absolutely free, and everybody benefits. Whether it's a formal or informal mentoring relationship, whether one day per month or one hour per week, for that hour or day it is all about *You*.

> *"A mentor is someone who allows you to see the hope inside yourself."*
> **Oprah Winfrey**

CHAPTER 8

THE ART OF NETWORKING

"Networking is marketing yourself, your uniqueness, and what you stand for."
Christine Comaford-Lynch

If you are serious about your career, learn how to network. Get out there and meet people in your work group, as well as people outside of your work group, department, or business line. You need to meet and interact with as many people as you can. These people may have networks of their own that you can tap into, which can help you reach your career goals. Get to know people, so people can get to know you. Networking takes time and effort, but it is well worth the benefits you may derive.

What is networking? Networking is the art of establishing and nurturing long-term, mutually beneficial relationships with the people you meet in your industry or area of interest, whether at industry conferences, at work, or online social networks. It is proactively taking charge of your career, building professional relationships, contacts, and getting them to know you and your abilities, skills, experiences, career aspirations, and interests.

Networking helps you work smarter, not harder. Working hard and spending time with your head down will help you focus on your work;

and most likely produce an exceptional work product. However, you should not be working so hard that you do not notice the day-to-day developments in your work environment. Unfortunately, working hard and doing your job well doesn't always guarantee the recognition and reward of your efforts. Keeping your head buried in your paperwork will not equal a promotion or career success. Networking with your peers, supervisors, their supervisors, and senior managers in your department and others throughout the company can make a difference. This is not to imply that you can be lax about the quality of your work. This means that you need to add networking to your to-do list. You need to produce an exceptional work product, make your boss look good, and make time to network.

Networking is a skill like any other and the more you do it, the better you become. It is about building professional relationships, contacts, and having those contacts know you. Career success is as much about what you know as it is about who you know.

How do you network?

Most networking begins through casual everyday meetings and conversations on an elevator, coffee line, professional conferences, or informal relationships with your colleagues, to name a few. However, many people find it difficult or do not feel comfortable going up to a person, introducing themselves, and making small talk.

What is small talk and how does it help? Small talk fills the voids in conversations, helps ease tense moments, sets others at ease, and helps us become acquainted with people we do not know. There are two ways to make small talk a little easier.

The first is to be well-informed and able to discuss general topics, which can include, but are not limited to, weather, news events, famous people, fitness crazes, travel, or sports. Develop and prepare your icebreaker, small talk opener. This should be something you feel comfortable saying and briefly discussing.

The second way to ease into small talk is by asking others about themselves, their family, work, or hobby, without getting personal. When making small talk, try to avoid any political or religious topics which you feel passionate about, as your view may be offensive to a person who does not share your opinion.

You can practice striking up a conversation with the people you meet in your day-to-day activities and normal routine. The more you practice making small talk, the more comfortable you will become. So, you must practice, practice, and then practice some more.

Some networking tips to keep in mind

Politically correct. The safest way to go is not to be too controversial and complaining. Outliers get labeled as too radical. Being too honest, blunt, or judgmental can hold you back or derail your career. Some things are better left unsaid.

Get to know people. Know and care for as many people as you can, even those who can't help progress your career. If you make others feel valued, important, and appreciated, chances are that these people will support you and your initiative sometime down the road. Learning to work well with and respect everyone is the best practice.

Join a professional group. If you are not comfortable with outright networking, volunteer or join a social group at work. Senior management often supports these groups, and this will give you access to mingle with other successful professionals in a more structured setting. It is an excellent venue to meet people outside of your department and business line.

Consider joining Toastmaster. Members of Toastmaster receive constructive evaluations and advice on networking and can help you build the confidence you need to network effectively.

Invite someone to lunch. Invite a potential mentor or a colleague that you would like to get to know better professionally for a lunch date. The relationships forged during a breakfast, lunch, or dinner meeting can be extremely beneficial for your career development. Start with some small talk to break the ice. Small talk will give you and your colleague the opportunity to get to know each other on a personal and professional level. Be respectful and remember that each encounter is an opportunity to learn and expand your network.

Developing your network

Creating a solid network is not simply meeting people, it requires that you get out and make connections with people that are open to developing a professional relationship with you. But where do you start? You can start with professional industry groups, join professional groups, work with nonprofits that support an area of interest to you, your peers can introduce you to like-minded people within your industry, or you can sign-up to attend networking events as an icebreaker and practice your networking skills.

Developing a network can be challenging and exhausting, especially when you network outside of your immediate work environment. The last thing you may want to do after a long day is attend an industry function. As challenging as networking can be, you can nourish, cultivate, and improve your networking skills over time as you develop a solid network and position as a successful professional. Networking, whether within or outside of your company, takes time and energy, but the benefits that you can gain from networking are worth the effort.

If you are interested in starting your own business or grow a small business, networking can help you generate leads. As people get to know you, they will become more comfortable doing business with you and eventually trust you and see you as a dependable person they can do business with. Networking will take time and effort, but can be an effective way to generate new leads for your business. During these networking sessions, your focus should be on informing others on what you and your business can offer and how this could be of value to them. Get business cards, contact information, so that you can follow up with folks and take the initial conversation to the next level.

Benefits of networking

Increased opportunities. By socializing with your peers and supervisors, you build trust and can often be privy to privileged information which can help position you for a career-enhancing opportunity. It can improve your professional image and visibility with senior management, further develop your areas of expertise, and improve your communication skills. These relationships can help you discover how to achieve your career goals, make career decisions, and help you develop a network.

Grow your network. The personal relationships you make at work will grow your network as you not only have a direct connection with your coworkers, but you also have indirect access to your coworkers' network, which increases your access to knowledge sharing.

Knowledge sharing: When your connections and your coworkers' connections share knowledge, you benefit from their experiences and can avoid some mistakes they've made or learn how to best handle a difficult work situation. In addition, as you share your knowledge and information with your contacts, you enhance your reputation and expertise with others.

Develop your professional image. Creating a network allows you to improve your professional image as you share your successes with your network. Networking provides the perfect venue for other professionals to get to know you and improve your career prospects.

The fact of the matter is that a strong professional network can enhance your career. Networking will give you a competitive edge throughout each stage of your career development as it will help you enhance required skills, stay on top of industry trends, meet potential mentors, clients, and other resources that will help in your career development.

Your career development is your responsibility, and it is up to you to develop the skills necessary for that next promotion or assignment. Networking within your company or industry organizations is an excellent venue for getting the lay of the land and increases your visibility with management, potential employer, and potential clients.

As you network, be your own campaign manager, and promote your most marketable and transferable skills, experiences, and expertise. You are in the best position to manage this campaign, if not you, then who? You know what you offer, what you bring to the table, so showcase it whenever you have the opportunity.

Add networking to your list of things to do because not only is it essential for you to get to know people, but people need to get to know you. So, toot your own horn, this is not bragging; it is marketing this product called *You*!

> *"Networking is not about just connecting people. It's about connecting people with people, people with ideas, and people with opportunities."*
> **Lee Iacocca**

CHAPTER 9
DISTINGUISH YOURSELF

"Brand yourself for the career you want, not the job you have."
Dan Schawbel

What do you want your legacy to be? How are you going to differentiate yourself? What is going to be your professional brand?

What is a personal brand?

Your brand is your essence, the unique energy you inject into everything you do, from the mundane to your most important initiative. It is your personal story which depicts those aspects of your personality that distinguish you from others and instills trust and credibility in your knowledge and your abilities.

You are in control of your personal brand. Perception is reality. Define and refine your personal brand so that you can enhance your marketability. Differentiate yourself and stand out from the competition.

Your personal brand distinguishes You

Developing a personal brand may sound challenging, but there are incremental steps you can take to build and promote your personal brand.

Identify your unique skills and strengths. Identify your unique and transferable skills and strengths so you can define and refine your personal brand and enhance your marketability. Identify and master the skills required in your field. Which of your unique skills will you choose to distinguish yourself and stand out from the competition?

Adopt a professional appearance. Ensure that you adopt a professional appearance. There are no written dress code standards within most organizations; however, there are certain unwritten expectations. Anyone who aspires to progress within their work environment needs to understand the importance of personal appearance. You only get one chance to make the right first impression, so don't blow it by ignoring your appearance.

Is it fair to judge a person's qualifications by what they wear? Of course not. But most of us judge people by their appearance. There is a time and a place for everything, and you need to ensure that you dress properly for your work environment. As campaign manager of your career, marketing that product called *You* to management and other decision makers, ensure that you dress appropriately as you never know who is going to judge you by your attire.

Women have many wardrobe alternatives and combination of accessories and others scrutinize their attire more so than men. Men quickly choose a shirt, tie, and business suit and they're ready to go. This is not to imply that men can't get it wrong or get away with dressing unprofessional. However, it can be much easier for women to cross the line from professional to unprofessional attire.

The decisions you make in the selection of your work attire can adversely affect your career. In my experience, management and others are paying attention to your appearance, and the way you dress can significantly impact your chances of getting that next promotion.

Inappropriate attire can also cause others not to take you seriously. When presenting or chairing a meeting, you want your colleagues and clients to focus on your message and not your anatomy, makeup, jewelry or fragrance. Be mindful of fragrances. You don't want your fragrance walking in before you, permeating the atmosphere, or leaving a trail when you walk away. You do not want people avoiding you because your fragrance adversely affects them.

You do not have to spend a lot of money to dress professionally. If you are in a corporate office environment, you can start off with two professional suits and other accessories that you can mix and match. Then build your wardrobe.

If you look and behave like a highly trained and wellgroomed professional, you will give yourself that competitive edge that may increase your chances when competing for that next promotion.

Identify your niche. A niche is an activity or expertise for which a person is best suited. In the workplace, this can be a job that you may be good at or a service you can make available to your clients. It can be an activity or talent that is innate and aligns with your personality and unique to you. By identifying your niche, you can focus your time and efforts on a certain career or particular market to target. It helps you stand out as a job candidate, secures work with ideal clients, and specifies your focus and talents.

Whether you want to start your own business or move to a new company, you need to identify your niche. You need to be specific about what distinguishes you from the competition, as it will help you create and develop a plan for your business or career.

Personal branding, why it matters

Self-confidence. Developing your personal brand gives you a sense of control and power as your management, peers, and clients perceive you as a well-connected and trusted person.

Self-awareness. Personal branding allows you to showcase your interests and skills to others. It gives you clear direction on where to take your career.

Trust and credibility. A strong personal brand will showcase your unique strengths and abilities, enhancing your marketability.

Establishes reputation. Personal branding refers to those aspects of your personality that distinguish you from your competition in the workplace. When management has to choose between you and another quality candidate with similar qualifications for a promotion or job assignment, your brand will help you stand out and may give you a competitive edge.

Showcase your talent. Your brand is your online portfolio. Branding yourself allows more people to get to know who you are and the value you bring to the organization.

Builds trust and credibility. Self-branding instills trust and credibility in your knowledge and your abilities, so your management or potential employer will know that you will be an excellent team member.

Highlights your Strengths. Your personal brand highlights your strengths. When cultivated well, your personal brand will signal to employers whether you'll be the right fit for an open role.

The truth about you

Your company hired you because someone saw something remarkable in you. They saw your potential. You exhibited some unique quality that attracted your company to hire you.

Your individuality got you hired, so leverage your personal style, values, and talents, and don't be shy about self-promoting them.

The specific job you perform today is most likely not a new position. Sure, there may have been some innovation along the way, but others have done the job before you. But here's what is new. This is the first time that the job is being done by *You* with your unique flare and personal attributes.

Personal branding is the act of using your occupation and personal attributes to promote your unique combination of skills, experience, and personality, what you want the world to see. It is how you tell your personal story.

I hope you can now answer the questions I asked at the beginning of the chapter. What do you want your legacy to be? How are you going to differentiate yourself? What is going to be your professional brand?

> *"Develop a standard for excellence.*
> *Without distinction there is extinction."*
> **Jon Michai**

CHAPTER 10

A MORE CONFIDENT YOU

"Inhale confidence, exhale doubt"
unknown author

Self-confidence is a belief in oneself, in one's abilities and judgment. Some people appear to be born with self-confidence, but most have to work at it. You can develop and nourish self-confidence. However, getting it right is a matter of striking a perfect balance between low-confidence and over-confidence that is realistic and represents your true ability.

Developing self-confidence from the outside-in

There are immediate steps you can take to develop into a more confident You from the outside-in. Focusing on your body language and your attire will give you an immediate edge and increase your confidence level.

Body language. One the most important thing you can do to develop a more confident *You* is to focus on your body language as it matters more than most people believe. Your responses to events are both external and internal as your subconscious and conscious responses come through in your use of language, tone of voice, appearance, and personal distance. Body language reveals in real time your state of mind through your gestures, postures, and physiological cues which broadcast your genuine feelings and intentions.

Body language is a natural, unconscious language that broadcasts your genuine feelings and intentions. It is most often the instinctive use of physical behavior, expressions, and mannerisms, giving and receiving wordless signals. All of your nonverbal behaviors—the gestures you make, the way you sit, how fast or how loud you talk, how close you stand, how much eye contact you make—send powerful messages.

Sometimes, what comes out of your mouth and what you communicate through your body language may be two totally different things. If you say one thing, but your body language says something else, your listener will probably feel you're being dishonest. When faced with mixed signals, the listener has to choose whether to believe your verbal or nonverbal message. When a conflict arises between your words and your body language, your body language wins every time.

How do you walk? Do you walk slow, tired, or energetic? Confident people walk quickly–they have places to go, people to see, and work to do. When *You* walk with a bounce in your step, you can control your thoughts, emotions, and influence others.

Think about your posture. Did you know that the way you sit tells a story, that people with lethargic movements display a lack of self-confidence? By practicing good posture, you'll automatically feel more confident. Attempt to practice good posture throughout your day. Roll your shoulders back, sit up straight and stand up tall.

Dress for success. *"When you look good, you feel good. Confidence with what you're wearing is very important. If you feel good, you will always perform your best without worrying about anything." Maria Sharapova*

Your attire speaks for you. This isn't being vain; it is about making you feel good about yourself. Develop your daily selfcare routine so that when you step out of your home, you are presenting the best version of *You*.

Developing self-confidence from the inside-out

There are things you can do to develop your self-confidence from the inside-out, whether you lack confidence in one specific area of your life or simply struggle to feel confident about anything.

Self-awareness. Some people don't realize they're lacking self-confidence. People that lack self-confidence have self-doubt, lack confidence in their abilities. The first step in becoming self-confident is to recognize that you are lacking self-confidence.

When you feel inadequate and useless, you sometimes attract circumstances, relationships, and situations that affirm that belief. Your body language will confirm your thoughts, and others will perceive your vulnerability and treat you as someone they can push around and who doesn't deserve respect.

Change your mindset. Changing long-held attitudes about yourself and your reactions to others is the best way to build your self-confidence. Develop positive thoughts and surround yourself with positive people. Are you choosing your thoughts or are your thoughts choosing you? If you drift into a negative mindset, stop whatever you are doing, take a deep breath, change your scenery by going for a walk, call someone that can talk you off of the ledge, play some music, or anything else that will break the chain of negative thoughts.

Benefits of developing your self-confidence

Being self-confident can positively impact your personal and professional relationships. A more confident you will perform better as you focus on the task at hand instead of worrying that you are not good enough. Having self-confidence and believing in yourself boosts your self-esteem and can lead to healthier relationships, as it gives you the strength to walk away from dysfunctional relationships. Self-confidence gives you the courage to step up and proactively apply for that promotion, volunteer to lead a team, or start your own business.

Self-confidence is one of the key ingredients required for a successful career. Projecting a lack of confidence and knowledge will construct barriers that may impede the growth of your career. Have faith in your skills and abilities and do not allow the cultural mantra of the organization, your cultural background, education, or your peers to affect your self-confidence.

Assess your self-worth not by one failure, one job, one relationship, success, or single experience. All of your experiences, both personal and professional, have made you the person you are today. Your worth is based on a conglomeration of experiences that helped you grow, mature, and develop into this product called *You*.

Be presumptuous enough to believe that you are just as good as, as smart as, or better than those around you and that you have a significant contribution to make. Don't talk yourself out of greatness. Lord knows that there are probably plenty of people around you who are already working on that.

> *"Believe in your infinite potential. Your only limitations are those you set upon yourself."*
> **Roy T. Bennett**

CHAPTER 11

BUSINESS ACUMEN – UNDERSTANDING THE BIG PICTURE

"Starting a business and building a product are not for the faint of heart. You have to learn to not let little disappointments get you down and to stay focused on the big picture."
Gillian Tans

The official definition of business acumen, according to Wikipedia, is "keenness and quickness in understanding and dealing with a 'business situation' (risks and opportunities) in a manner that is likely to lead to a good outcome."

Business acumen is not any one particular skill, but a collection of competencies, knowledge, and awareness of multiple aspects of a particular business. It is an ability that allows you to understand and cope with unique business situations. It's knowing how all the pieces work together, understanding the how, when, where and why of your current position and its impact on the day-to-day operations of your company.

Taking your career beyond certain levels within any organization requires that you develop business acumen. Developing business acumen is a complex topic which can take more than one chapter to grasp. But in its simplest terms, it is understanding how the different moving parts of the company work together to make it successful.

Most employees handle a specific area of the business and have little understanding of the impact their work and daily decisions have on other areas of their company. In order to make effective decisions, it is necessary to understand the big picture. You should know and understand how your organization runs at every level so that you can make informed decisions. At the very least, you need to understand the business model. How does your company operate? How do they make money? How does your role impact the business?

Besides figuring out how your position, group, or department functions, it's also important to get a glimpse into how other groups outside of your department work. No employee or department operates in a vacuum, so it's important for you to understand the priorities of the surrounding people. Understanding their priorities will help you better collaborate with them and can help you successfully propose and execute joint initiatives.

Why it matters

You are an important link in the chain responsible for a specific area of the business. Everyone around you depends on you to not only hold up, but to fortify your link of the chain. You can fortify your link by understanding the objectives of your unit, section, department, and company. Understand the impact of your work and the decisions you make on areas that are beyond your immediate scope.

You may think to yourself, "Why bother? Why should I care?" You should care because every role within your organization is interdependent, like the links of a chain. Why bother? Because looking at the big picture helps you understand the interdependence and how the moving pieces come together, giving you a glimpse of what is out in the horizon for the company, your unit, your group, and even your career.

The only way to know where you can take your career is to understand and know what is out there. And that starts with understanding the big picture, developing business acumen. Developing business acumen will increase your value and contribute to the success and bottom line of your company.

Understanding the bigger picture of your department and organization will help you make better judgments, decisions, find solutions, and project a higher level of confidence, as it gives you a greater sense of purpose.

Developing business acumen

Some may argue that business acumen applies to analytical and senior positions, stressing the need for understanding of internal and external corporate drivers, such as the markets, competition, organizational drivers, products, and the financial strategy of the company. But what if I told you that business acumen can apply to any position within any company? Developing business acumen competency isn't just for those in leadership positions. The skill can extend to everyday scenarios, improving your efficiency at your job or being able to solve challenging problems at work.

Developing your business acumen takes time and requires that you change the way you view your job and how you apply the knowledge you've gained. Over time, you will master key terms and accumulate a wealth of knowledge that will take your career to new heights. Below are some incremental steps you can take to develop and strengthen your business acumen:

Prioritize. Focus on the items that make a difference in your business and area of expertise within the business. By prioritizing the items you focus on during the day will allow you to be much more productive.

Understand the consequences. Decisions have consequences. There is always a trade-off in decision-making and understanding the consequence of each option will make it easier to weigh each potential outcome and make an informed decision.

Problem-solving. Apply your knowledge to solve business problems. You do this by collecting relevant information about a situation to assess solutions, then apply your understanding of the consequences to choose a course of action that has the highest likelihood to achieve your objectives.

Business model. The better you understand the key metrics that are important to the success of your company's ability to generate revenue, the greater your understanding of the consequences of your business decisions. Understanding the various factors will develop and fortify your business acumen.

Educated yourself. You can educate yourself through independent reading, online courses, training offered by your organization, or any other means you find works for you. When you devote time to educating yourself, you'll find marketing ideas, best practices for a work process, innovative technological ideas, changing business and industry trends. There is an unlimited list of topics that can enhance your business acumen. The best thing educating yourself will do is train your brain to absorb and use the data to help you better understand the business.

Volunteer your participation. Taking an active role in company projects, committees, or special initiatives will help you gain a deeper understanding of how your company operates.

Get a mentor. Find and work with a mentor to help you better understand the ins and outs of the company so that you can learn more about their experience and the knowledge they possess on how the company operates.

Benefits of developing business acumen

In order to make effective decisions, it is necessary for you to understand the big picture. Why? Because everything is related and you are merely a link in a chain of required tasks that make the organization successful. In any business, it is necessary for each person to perform specific roles and functions with each aspect of the business relying on the other. Most people only focus on their specific roles, without considering how they affect the other departments. Looking at the big picture allows you to see how everything works together.

Understand business decisions. Developing stronger business acumen–or understanding of the big picture will give you a clearer picture and logic of underlying business decisions and help you better understand important company communications and data, including financial statements which will lead you to use that knowledge to make better decisions.

Competitive advantage. Developing strong business acumen can give you a competitive advantage as you are better positioned to problem-solve and contribute to the company's bottom line as you deepen your understanding of how actions and decisions impact key company measures and leadership objectives.

Enhances communications skills. You will effectively communicate ideas to other employees, managers, executives, and you will represent yourself and your ideas in an informed professional manner. It will give you the knowledge you need to take part in discussions of a financial or business nature with your peers, management, and other decision makers.

Improve decision-making. You'll make informed decisions and pivot effectively when your strategy requires a change in plans, increasing your chances of success.

Business acumen requires that you proactively devote your time and attention to its development. You must expose yourself to a diverse and wide breadth of experiences, education, and resources to support your growth and development in this area. Strong business acumen can give you a better understanding of business issues, adapt and remain flexibleduring challenging times, greater comprehension of business operations, which enables you to provide insight into achieving goals and ensuring success.

> *"Big-picture thinkers broaden their outlook by striving to learn from every experience. They don't rest on their successes; they learn from them."*
> **John C. Maxwell**

CHAPTER 12

QUALITY OVER QUANTITY

"Yesterday is history, tomorrow is a mystery. And today? Today is a gift. That's why we call it the present."
B. Olatunji

A new job or reassignment within your company can be stressful and daunting. No one expects you to know everything as you walk in the door. Don't be afraid to ask the what, why, and how of your new job. Understanding your role, responsibilities, and expectations will improve your performance.

Success-minded employees understand the importance of honing their skills and expertise. Take the time to identify any skills, knowledge, or on-the-job training that will enhance your work performance. Do not wait for your boss to point out your deficiencies and recommend training and conferences that you should attend during a performance review.

Once you have clarified your role and deliverables, stay focused on what is right in front of you. This way, you can master your current assignment and continue to build and capitalize on the knowledge of the previous one. View each assignment as a building block that will solidify the foundation of your career and will help propel you forward to that next plateau.

If you are in a large corporation, you will have many departments and career paths to choose from. As you move from one department to the next, there is always a new culture and lingo to learn. Even though you are in the same company, the differences in the customs, mindsets, and focuses of the distinct groups will amaze you.

Unfortunately, longevity in the corporate environment does not equal promotion. Years on the job do not automatically qualify or entitled you to a promotion. Are your contributions creating value? In order words, can you point to any recent significant achievement or milestone that supports your advancement?

When you master your current assignment, you give your boss a reason to promote you for excellent results. Learn how to set priorities when facing many tasks during the day so that you focus on what is most important in your job. Speed and dependability in the completion of an assignment is a valuable trait.

The ability to work under pressure and manage your time is essential as many jobs come with demanding deadlines that can cost the company money. You need to develop a decisive attitude, the ability to think clearly, and set stress aside so you can work well within tight deadlines.

Early in my career, I learned that quality is just as or more important as quantity. In one of my many work groups, there was a gentleman that had an extremely light workload compared to others in the group. When asked how it was possible that this person could get away with doing so little compared to what others were producing, senior management responded, "It is true that he does very little, but the little he does, he does exceedingly well." Lesson learned quality over quantity; never underestimate the value of producing an exceptional work product.

Staying focused and mastering each assignment without worrying about the ones that would follow was my approach. I knew I had to master my current assignment. I had to let that next assignment take care of itself as I showed my abilities and continued to build on the knowledge of the previous assignment.

I learned the petroleum business from the ground up, and with each new assignment, I was building and capitalizing on the knowledge of the previous one. I viewed each assignment as a building block that solidified the foundation of my career and would help me achieve my goal to move to the next assignment.

From 1982 to 1992, every job I had done was clerical and, although not sufficiently challenging, served as an excellent venue for learning the fundamentals of our industry. I spent the first ten years of my corporate career paying my dues and learning as much as I could about the energy business.

I had to work twice as hard as everyone else to prove that I could do the job. It meant not letting anything slip and reading every single piece of paper that came across my desk. I was constantly researching and educating myself on how my job fit into the bigger scheme of things. I wanted to make sure that I was making a difference and contributing to the bottom line.

My modus operandi was to be consistent in my performance simultaneously, working on increasing my responsibilities by mastering and capitalizing on every assignment, learning and thoroughly understanding the priorities of our business. No job was too big or small. It did not matter to me that some assignments were not glorious; some were quite mundane, but I knew that even the smallest action within each assignment was educating and propelling me forward toward the next assignment and level.

Never undermine or underestimate a strong work ethic, because productivity and the bottom line are the primary concerns. If you master your current assignment, it is likely that management will have confidence in your ability to achieve more.

Your ability to make your boss look good is priceless. When your boss can give you an assignment and walk away confident that you will get it completed on time and, to the company's satisfaction, you will significantly elevate your value within the organization.

Take it one assignment at a time and celebrate each accomplishment along the way. Give yourself credit for a job well done.

Yesterday is in the past, and it is exactly where it belongs, behind you, and tomorrow is not here yet. You cannot hope for a perfect past, but you can certainly work on a much better tomorrow by developing the skills and knowledge required for that next assignment today.

"The future depends on what you do today."
Mahatma Gandhi

PART II

NAVIGATING THE WORK ENVIRONMENT

CHAPTER 13

LARGE CORPORATION OR SMALL COMPANY?

"Corporate culture is the only sustainable competitive advantage that is completely within the control of the entrepreneur."
David Cummings, Co-Founder, Pardot

Choosing whether to work for a large or small company can affect the quality of your life.

When deciding on where you will eventually work, keep in mind that you will most likely spend more time with your coworkers than with your biological or nuclear family. Your place of employment will become your home away from home; your coworkers will become your extended family.

Unlike your biological or nuclear family, you can choose the people and the environment you work in. So, make sure that you fit in the environment and that it is a place where you can visualize yourself flourishing in a rewarding and successful career. There's no right or wrong answer for which is better. You must evaluate the advantages and disadvantages of both and make the best decision for you and your family.

Small company

Small companies are fast-paced, mostly privately owned, often focus on a niche market, and have fewer than five hundred employees. When working with a small company, you can be a 'big fish in a small pond', as it offers a much better chance of being recognized through your daily interactions with senior management.

Some benefits of working at a small company

Well-rounded experience. Being fast paced can make it easier to excel on the job, as employees can get involved in a variety of projects and gain well-rounded experience. Employees can get involved in different aspects of the business, from social media/ content strategist to human resource representative in which you can develop a range of skills you may not have learned otherwise.

Develop business acumen. The chances of working closely with company leaders are much greater, which can help you develop your business acumen skills, as you will undoubtedly have to understand the financials and operations of the business in order to engage in fruitful conversation with your management and peers.

Faster promotions. The involvement and interaction in major projects and your involvement in some of the administrative aspects of running the company can get the decision-makers to know you, your abilities, and aspirations. If you are a strong performer, you are likely to get faster promotions and pay raises.

Encourage creativity. Small companies encourage out of the box thinking and management supports and champions new ideas on how to improve the business or a process. Encouraging a creative thinking environment fosters collaboration as team members bond during the process. Individual employees also feel a sense of inclusion, respect, and accomplishment as they feel their opinion and abilities are valued.

Familial environment. Small companies foster a nurturing, familiar environment. Employees form close working relationships, which can at times feel like your extended family. Employees know and understand each other's nuances and tend to be more supportive and understanding during a coworkers' personal or professional difficulties.

Some downsides of a small company

Career development. You may have to settle for having a job and not a career. Small companies have a flat organizational structure which limits career paths available to pursue. In order to get that coveted position, you may have to wait for the company to decide to expand and create a new position. If a new position isn't forthcoming, then you may have to wait for someone to retire, quit, or die. If you do not want to wait, then your only option is to leave the company.

Lower revenue. Smaller companies have less cash on hand as they generate less revenue. This translates into smaller raises, older equipment and furniture, not working with the latest technology, and fewer resources to support employee programs.

Smaller benefits packages. Some small companies do not provide health insurance but may offer a small stipend to help cover some costs of purchasing on your own. If they do provide health insurance, you may end up paying a higher out of pocket for medical services, as the number of employees does not get them the best deal with insurance companies. You are also less likely to find a small company that offers retirement plan, pension, tuition reimbursement and other perks offered at larger companies.

Less job security. A natural disaster such as COVID, economic downturn, loss of a major client, layoffs, cost cutting initiatives, or other event beyond the control of the company, can cause a small company to go under as they may not have the resources to stay afloat.

Large corporations

In a large corporation, you are a small fish in the vast ocean. Large corporations have two thousand or more employees competing to climb the corporate ladder. It is, therefore, much easier to get lost in the shuffle of employees.

Corporations, like people, have distinct personalities, and no amount of hard work and determination will help you get ahead if you are in the wrong corporate culture. The culture of an organization is its personality, its core values and beliefs that can affect your career satisfaction and success. Sometimes, the culture is implied, but in others, there are formal standards that define the corporate ethics, beliefs, and expected behavior of employees.

Some advantages of Large Corporations

Boundless professional opportunities. Career opportunities within a large corporation are boundless. You can learn, grow, and expand your horizons, all within the same company. Some large corporations comprise several companies under the same umbrella, giving employees the ability to transfer from one to the other and providing access to new locations, people, and opportunities.

Career development. Large corporations have a structured career development program that you can use to manage your career. Get familiar with the company's specific set of rules for evaluations, raises, and promotions so you can develop an informed career plan for your next move.

Job security. Many people choose to work at large corporations for the benefits and job security. Large companies provide a stable work environment, and the growth of the company largely depends on the team spirit of the workforce. While any company can find itself on the wrong side of the economy, large companies are in a better position to weather the economic storm. Chances are that you won't suddenly find yourself out of a job. But, if you do, the company will offer a severance package to help you transition to another job.

Higher starting salary. Larger companies offer a higher starting salary as compared to smaller companies. However, salary increments, bonuses, and promotions are usually linked to your individual performance and the financial performance of the company.

Continuous learning. Encourages continuous learning by providing a variety of training programs designed to develop and sharpen your skills and technical knowledge of the industry. This free skill development is something that you can take advantage of as you develop your career plan. Education or new skill set is invaluable. If things do not work out as you planned, you can always take that new skill with you to another company.

Business travel. Many large corporations have an international presence and network which may allow you to travel to countries you would probably not try (or could not afford) to visit.

Lots of perks. Most large companies offer both medical and life insurance options for you and your family. The larger the company, the better the deal they will negotiate with insurance companies, which translates into a better rate and out-of-pocket expenses for their employees. Many also offer tuition reimbursement, pension, 401k savings plan matches, and other fringe benefits.

Zero tolerance. Most corporations have zero tolerance for unethical behavior, and ignorance of the law, rule, or regulation is no excuse. The company expects employees to conduct themselves and business in a way that positively affects the reputation of the company, the bottom line, and the stakeholders who have a vested interest in the corporation.

As in our society, ethical behavior is a common expectation in the corporate world. The corporation expects its employees to conduct business ethically, always recognizing what is right and wrong. In both cases, it is your responsibility to distinguish between right and wrong. Learning that distinction in your corporate environment is extremely critical, as failure to do so can cost you your career or job.

Employees and shareholders also expect their executives to behave and manage the company ethically. Unethical behavior erodes the confidence of the public, employees, and stockholders. It also makes the public skeptical about the ethics of corporate America. It creates an overall distrust, as the public thinks, "*What else are they hiding? How many others are out there duping the public, their employees, and stakeholders?*"

Creating and sustaining an ethical environment is a long and continuous journey in both your personal behavior and how you conduct business. So, if there is even a hint of impropriety in a proposed action, stop and rethink your position before proceeding.

Some disadvantages of working in a large company Forced ranking. A somewhat controversial tool used by large organizations to identify the company's best and worst performing employees, using person-to-person comparisons. The aim of the forced ranking is to segregate the workforce into three tiers: the top 20 percent represent the future leaders, the middle 70 percent are consistently solid performers, and the bottom 10 percent represent those that are perceived to contribute the least. Forced ranking affects salary raises, promotions, and bonuses.

Survival of the fittest. The large corporate can be dog-eat-dog. This survival-of-the-fittest environment can be even more extreme if you work at the corporate headquarters. When it comes time for promotions, more coworkers will compete with you for that promotion. The corporate arena can be an extremely competitive environment, as hard work alone or longevity in the company may not be sufficient for that next promotion. You need to understand and abide by all the written and unwritten rules of the organization, as there may be a specific structure delineating the requirements.

Bureaucratic. Most large corporations are highly bureaucratic with clear hierarchies, formal, rigid division of labor and strict policies which can inhibit productivity, diminish innovation and decrease morale. The strict policies slow down the process as they are laden with specific rules and regulations requiring approval from several levels of management before implementing an initiative.

Impersonal environment. Large corporations can be cold and impersonal, where you only really get to know a fraction of the other employees. You won't know everyone, and everyone won't know you. Although you are part of a large organization, you may feel like a cog in the wheel, functionally necessary but of small significance or importance within the larger organization.

Whether you decide to work at a small or large organization, select a company that fits your goals and needs. Weigh the pros and cons of working with both small and large organizations so you end up at a company where you can thrive.

In addition to asking your prospective employer all the relevant benefits questions to make sure that they meet your family's needs, ask yourself the follow questions:

- Can I see myself in this environment for the next five, ten, or fifteen years?

- Does this company appreciate its employees and their contributions?
- Does the company offer ample opportunities for career development and upward mobility?
- What is the proportion of women and minorities in leadership positions and what is their role?
- Which behaviors does management reward and frown upon?
- Do I agree with the company's ethics?
- Is the corporate structure too stifling?
- Will I succeed in a formal or an informal environment, a small company versus a large corporation?

You cannot afford to underestimate the importance of ensuring that your personal values align with your employer's values, as this alignment will directly impact and influence your productivity, satisfaction, and opportunities within the company. I've seen many people throughout the years who did not have this alignment, and the work appeared to be much harder than what it truly was. They hated their jobs and were utterly miserable as they were constantly striving to be something they were not losing their sense of self and identity.

As you assess your company or a prospective employer, make sure you fully understand the environment and culture you are seeking. Ensure that there is alignment between your core values and the company's. If they are not, chances are you will not achieve your career goals and aspirations.

Take the time to evaluate your prospective or current organization to ensure that you fully understand the culture so you can flourish in a rewarding and successful career.

> *"If you do not manage culture, it manages you, and you may not even be aware of the extent to which this is happening."*
> **Edgar Schein, Professor MIT School of Management**

CHAPTER 14

MANAGING A BAD MANAGER

Abusive, nasty, obnoxious people exist in every facet of life. They are in every company and industry. They are in our families, neighborhoods, and workplaces. These people can easily wear you out, frustrate you, and make your life miserable. They are bullying, intrusive, and controlling; and will rarely provide constructive feedback. They are glory hogs who will take credit for your work and will not support you during a crisis.

Dictionary.com defines the word power as "the possession of control or command over others". These managers let the power of their leadership position go to their heads. They do not use their power; they abuse it, which results in coercive and bullying behavior. Managers have a choice to use or abuse the power the organization has granted them. Sadly, too many choose to abuse that power.

Many of us have experienced working under a bad manager. In addition to the abusive, bullying type, bad managers can also be control freaks that micro-manage and nitpick at everything you do. They can be paternalistic, managing their employees as if they were children, believing that they know what is in the best interest of the employees. They can be overbearing and condescending, giving feedback in an abusive and demoralizing fashion. They can be two-faced telling their employees one thing but behaving in a way that only benefits their own career. They set unreasonable levels of expectations for their staff. They can be non-supportive of their employees throwing them under the bus when things go wrong. They have poor communication and leadership skills, which results in a lack of guidance for the staff. These are just a few examples of some characteristics of a poor manager; the actual list can be quite extensive. I'm sure that you can name a few based on your experience and perspective.

One management style does not work for all employees, and what may appear to be an appropriate approach for one person will not work for the next. However, there are some managers that everyone agrees to be horrendous managers with zero interpersonal skills, and no one quite understands how or why they are still managing people.

In fact, many employees have moved on to new companies or departments just to get away from a terrible boss. Leaving the company on a sour note feeling abused, over-worked, under-appreciated, and under-paid. Many walk-away from well-paying jobs, excellent benefits, and even their pension, all because of one lousy manager that management has failed to deal with. In these extreme cases, many employees feel so stressed that they leave to preserve their health and sanity. The years of service for those that choose to walk away can vary as everyone's situation differs based on their tolerance and level of patience. For most, it is the best decision they have ever made, and the one regret is not having decided sooner.

There are others that have had their careers derailed or obliterated by a terrible manager, but decided to stay with the company. Some stay hoping for transfer or promotion out of the department of their boss. For some, it could be age, years of service, or the inability to duplicate their current salary, benefits package, and pension. People choose to stay for various reasons that depend on their particular situation.

There is no single solution when deciding to quit or stick it out, as each person's situation is unique. The final decision is highly personal that takes many factors into consideration. You must make the best decision you can under your particular circumstance. The key is to remain true to yourself and your goals.

Surviving a negative work environment

Unless you are independently wealthy, chances are you can't do without your job. So, how do you defend yourself against the attacks of a bad manager while preserving your sanity, dignity, and career? How do you handle a terrible boss that constantly undermines you and your abilities?

You must first accept the fact that your boss is in charge and managing your career, which makes the situation much harder to manage. It is a fact of your work life that you have to answer to your boss. If your intention is to develop and grow a career within the company, then you need to figure out a way to get along with your boss or learn to work around his less-than-supportive behavior.

So, instead of lashing out, which in most cases will work against you, or lodging a complaint with your human resource department, maintain your professionalism and attempt to resolve the problem yourself. Some suggested strategies can include:

Network. Build relationships with other senior employees or managers so that they can get to know you and your abilities. Broadening your network will help thwart any negative feedback from your boss.

Enhance your credibility. Keep up your work ethic by meeting your commitments and deadlines. Remain diligent in your daily duties. Do not do or say anything that your boss can use against you. Try to be the perfect employee.

Don't over-promise and under-deliver. Do not take on more responsibility than you can realistically handle. If you do not deliver on your commitments, your boss will most likely use this against you, regardless of your efforts and intentions.

Understand the objectives and expectations. Prioritize your daily tasks to ensure that you meet your manager's expectations. Review your prioritized to-do list with your boss to ensure that he agrees with your priorities. Discussing and documenting your priorities will minimize the potential for misunderstanding on your deliverables.

Minimize personal contact. To the extent possible, minimize personal contact with your manager. Is it possible to communicate via e-mail or voice mail? Minimizing direct contact may reduce the opportunity for confrontation with your boss.

Kill him with kindness. Disarm him with unexpected polite behavior; You'll confuse him and he may not know what to make of your reaction. Hopefully, he will stop and think about what he has just said or done. Sometimes people say or do things for effect, to get a certain reaction out of you. Try not to give in to this manipulation of your psyche.

Give him the benefit of the doubt. Try to give your boss the benefit of the doubt. Do you believe his actions are intentional or malicious? Or is he the type of the person who just does not realize how he is coming across? Few people make an honest self-assessment of their behavior and without constructive feedback, will remain oblivious to their unprofessional and unsupportive behavior. A study based on surveys and interviews with 200 plus managers in approximately 40 countries concluded that most ineffective leaders remain blissfully unaware of the harm they do to their organizations. The study also found that overall, only 35 percent of respondents at high performing companies said their leaders were doing a good job inspiring their teams. (Thunderbird School of Global Management *When bosses do harm: Breaking the hindrance trap, by* Kannan Ramaswamy, Ph.D., and Bill Youngdahl, Ph.D.)

Fully assess the situation. Try to assess the situation from all angles, including what *You* may have contributed to the situation. Then, take the high road with as much patience, perseverance, and professionalism as you can muster. This can be a daunting task that is much easier said than done.

- Once you have fully assessed the situation, take immediate steps to rectify the problem. Schedule a meeting with your boss to let him know your understanding of the situation. Prepare talking points for your meeting, as this will ensure that you stay focused on the relevant issues.

- Address your concerns in a professional, polite, focused, and calm manner. Being rude and unprofessional is counterproductive and will not help you meet your goals and objectives. A frank, polite, and professional discussion can go a long way.

- Addressing your concerns with your boss may also backfire and make things worse. However, instead of sitting on the sidelines silently suffering from his abusive behavior, you should at least attempt to address the situation. At least you will have the satisfaction of knowing that you took actionable steps to remedy the situation instead of being a victim.

- You never know how someone is going to react, and your boss may just surprise you. Most people carry around their own fears, weaknesses, and idiosyncrasies; and given the opportunity, most will try to do better. Your boss may just walk away with renewed respect for you for having the courage to stand up for yourself professionally.

Sometimes, you may have to agree to disagree, and that is okay too.

Documenting the situation

If the problem you are facing is of a more serious nature, which you believe may require human resource or legal intervention, then you should document the situation. Documenting your situation means writing all the details and keeping any memos, letters, e-mails, or voice mails that can support your position. This documentation is essential for filing grievances should the gravity of the situation escalate and require a paper trail to support your case in a formal internal or external hearing.

- Fully document, in chronological order, all the relevant factors that support your position, while the facts are fresh in your mind.
- Use full names, title, and position within the company of all involved in the situation and any potential witnesses that can support your position.
- Stick to the facts by focusing on *who, what, where,* and *when.* Resist the temptation to speculate on *why* the situation may have occurred.
- Consult an employment lawyer for the more extreme cases.

Going up against management or the company is not for the faint of heart. The formal grievance process can be a daunting task that can be extremely stressful and difficult to endure. However, you will increase your chances of prevailing if you present a well-supported, objectively written, and thoroughly documented case in your defense.

Difficult work situations ebb and flow in intensity, so assess your situation and take the action steps warranted by the circumstances.

If after your best efforts to resolve the issue, you see no evidence of improvement in your situation, and you still want to stay with the company, you may consider a transfer out of your department, as a last resort. If you decide to transfer, do not bad-mouth your manager or peers to your replacement or new colleagues. Try not to burn any bridges. Leave with as much dignity, honor, and grace as you can muster by fulfilling your commitments to your department before you leave.

Don't become an emotional hostage

When someone's behavior triggers so much anguish, you may hold resentment toward that person, maybe even daydreaming of how to get even. Holding on to resentment makes you an emotional hostage to the other person, as it consumes your energy, enthusiasm, and effectiveness. These people are unhappy in their own lives, and it is often said that misery loves company.

Don't allow yourself to become an emotional hostage. I spent many years hating an abusive manager, and honestly, it was not worth it. I wish I would've had someone to counsel and coach me on the art of forgiving and letting go.

Forgive the person, let go of the resentment, let it roll off of your back, and walk away. Letting go will free you from the hostage situation. The benefits derived from forgiving will be a much better option than harboring resentment and suffering any adverse consequence because of acting rashly or in revenge. It is not worth the time and energy such people require.

Let it go and free yourself from the mental hold this person has imposed. If you do not let go, you will remain trapped in your own world of misery.

While you probably cannot change an ineffective manager, the good news is that you can learn from a terrible boss. You can learn how *not* to manage. You can learn how to recognize inappropriate behavior. You have a living example of how a bad manager behaves. This is behavior you do not want to emulate. As a leader, you want to use, not abuse, the power granted to you.

Deciding to learn something from a difficult situation is the best strategy for coping with adversity. Ask yourself what you can learn from this situation. People will come in and out of your life for a specific purpose. Try not to miss the lesson and the growth opportunity that life has provided you through this relationship and experience. Regard everyone you meet as a co-star in the movie of your career. Every stage of your journey has helped you become stronger, wiser, more patient, resilient, and experienced. Your current situation is simply another stage that brings an opportunity to learn and continue growing.

Change is a certainty in life, and that includes the workplace. The corporate environment is just like the weather; if you wait long enough, things will change. So, try to weather the storm as best you can. Instead of being this bad manager's victim, become his apprentice. Take control by choosing to make the adverse situation part of your informal education.

A Rocky Start to My Corporate Career

I started my corporate career with Mobil Oil Corporation in 1982 at the age of twenty-five after working as a legal secretary in Midtown Manhattan for six years. I had seven years of marriage, three young children, and I was still working on my undergraduate degree in International Business Management at Pace University.

The six years I spent at the law firm were my formative years. The office was my home away from home, and the people became part of my extended family. Leaving the law firm was one of the hardest things I've had to do. I started out at the young age of nineteen, naïve, childless, and rough around the edges. I left at twenty-five, much more poised, refined, and with three children. I still had some maturing and polishing to achieve, but my smarts, skills, work ethics, and talents compensated for my lack of tact.

This was a significant turning point in my life. I felt like the little bird that ultimately has to leave its nest and venture into the world on its own.

The difference between the corporate environment and a small law firm is like night and day. The law firm had fewer than thirty employees. It offered a nurturing, familial environment. It was a fast-paced environment, where I worked on a variety of projects and gained well-rounded experience. I was much more than a legal secretary, as it required me to provide a wide range of secretarial, administrative, and office management duties.

The corporate environment was immense and impersonal, and its inner workings eluded me. Initially, I was not sure this bureaucratic environment was for me. Fortunately, the law firm had left its doors open for me. I always had the option to go back if the job with Mobil did not work out.

Besides the differences between the two environments and culture, the duties required were as stark. Accustomed to the intellectual stimulation of the work at the law firm, I found the secretarial job with Mobil quite dull. The daily duties required typing short telexes, delivering mail, and running some personal errands for the manager. Yuck!

Still, having a less demanding full-time job had its benefits. One advantage was being able to do my schoolwork during the day. In this position, I could complete my work and help the other secretaries with their work in a matter of hours.

One other significant advantage was the tuition reimbursement offered by the corporation, which eased the financial burden of tuition. This corporate benefit enabled me to take as many classes as I could handle instead of only enrolling in the classes I could afford.

Despite the benefits, my corporate experience with Mobil had a rocky start. Once again, the universe was testing my resolve. Besides struggling with balancing a budget, taking care of a family, and being a part-time college student, they assigned me to work for a less-than-supportive, emotionally abusive, mean-spirited, anal-retentive boss.

On more than one occasion, I saw a different person walking out of his office in tears. In fact, one of the professional women in our group, who was in the United States on foreign assignment, quit the company because of his abusive behavior. From what I could surmise, senior management was aware of this abusive behavior and did absolutely nothing about it. In fact, they seemed to reward him with one promotion after another.

What truly mattered to the management at the time were the results, regardless of how people were being treated. Everyone seemed to ignore his less than professional behavior, as he was knowledgeable and savvy about the business and producing results. If only he had been as effective at managing his interpersonal skills.

Fortunately for me and my sanity, this horrendous situation lasted a little less than six months, as senior management promoted the abusive manager to his next assignment of terror. However, before he left our department, he recommended my termination at the end of the six-month probationary period. The quality of my work was not the issue; it was that I had the audacity to stand up to him and not tolerate his abusive behavior. If he pushed me, I pushed back harder. I'd go toe to toe with him, and he was not accustomed to anyone standing up to him, especially not a low-level secretary who had just walked through the door, such as myself. He hated that I dared to defend myself and that I would not let him break my spirit and resolve.

He once said to me, "You are wasting your time by going to Pace University and thinking that you are going to go up even one rung of the corporate ladder. I will make sure that no one in this company touches you with a ten-foot pole."

I responded, "Mobil is not the only company hiring."

I do not know what he told the manager who replaced him, but I got the distinct impression that the man was apprehensive as I approached to introduce myself. Whatever he said to the new manager did not work. This new manager and I got along exceptionally well. In fact, he was extremely impressed with my skills and work ethic and became one of my biggest supporters and one of my informal mentors.

After the six-month probationary period, with the unwavering support of my manager, I became an official employee. Things were looking brighter. The dark cloud that had followed me suddenly lifted.

I could now start working on a plan to achieve my first goal: to get out of the secretarial position. This was not commonplace, especially for someone new to the organization. I could honestly have retired five years earlier if I had a dime for every time I was told I was wasting my time by working toward my bachelor's degree. Many claimed that the company would never recognize a part-time degree, work efforts, or give me the opportunity to move out of the secretarial position. I did not let that discourage me. In fact, I saw it as a challenge.

I knew that getting ahead in this corporate environment would not be easy, but I was determined to put in the time required to get ahead.

"The secret to success is to start from scratch and keep on scratching."
Dennis Green

CHAPTER 15

EMBRACE CHANGE

"Change is inevitable, growth is intentional."
Glenda Cloud

Embracing change means effectively managing our perceptions and fears. Change is the natural circle of life that brings about progress. Even though we can intellectualize that change is inevitable, we fight to keep the status quo, we try to hang on to what is most familiar. Clinging to the way things used to be may give a person a sense of security, but growth and progress can only come when we embrace change and accept the new opportunities and possibilities that come with new beginnings.

Everyone perceives change differently. Some react positively, with renewed energy and excitement, while others have a more pessimistic view and perceive the change as the beginning of the end for them. As a result, they become stressed, overwhelmed, and sometimes bitter individuals.

If the change is our idea, we embrace it enthusiastically, excited about the possibilities. However, if someone imposes the change, we rebel and resist adapting to change.

We need to learn to embrace change as a normal part of our lives and stop fighting with ourselves and the establishment. Our reaction, attitude, and perception of the change will either hold us back or propel us to new heights.

When Mobil merged with Exxon, many of Exxon's senior management and employees moved into our headquarters building. To me, it felt as though we had sold our home with the opportunity to continue living in the guest room. We lost the master bedroom, master bath, and someone else was calling the shots. We no longer had any say in how, when, and where of things. It was a strange feeling. It was a confusing and emotional time in all of our lives.

During the transition period, what people feared the most was the unknown, the uncertainty of how things were going to be. There were many uncertainties about the organizational structure, the company's business strategy, operating practices, routines, roles, and responsibilities. Many employees had to interview for their current positions. Stress was at an all-time high and morale at an all-time low.

Many of the employees lost their sense of purpose, self-esteem, credibility, and sense of security. If not managed correctly, these emotions can be difficult to overcome, since we can be our own worst enemy and unwittingly sabotage our progress with negative thoughts and ideas. When the change involves a perceived personal loss, the process becomes much more complex and harder to overcome as you go through periods of denial, anger, depression, and finally acceptance.

Suggested strategies

Manage your perceptions. Change does not have to be stressful, overwhelming, or confusing if you manage your perceptions and fears. The transition period from the old to the new is the time to figure out how you will fit into the new organization. This is the perfect time to revisit your life and career and clearly delineate what you want and envision for yourself. Get a feel for the new organization and how you will fit in. This may require that you leave some of the old ways that no longer fit behind.

Plan ahead. Stay alert and focus on how the work changes are being implemented. Some will be gradual, while others will be immediate. Is the organization creating new jobs, is there an opportunity for a new position or even a promotion because of the reorganization? Do these organizational changes involve learning a new skill? If so, what can you do to prepare and position yourself for a new assignment or promotion? Expecting changes in your work environment will help you plan and identify any training or resource that will help you better assimilate into the new organization.

Current work process. Review current work processes to determine whether there is a need for enhancement, elimination, or whether they will work well within the new work environment. Then, review your findings and potential solutions with the management team, letting them know which processes worked well, which were highly deficient, and which will no longer fit into the new organization.

Opportunity to make a fresh start. View the change as an opportunity to make a fresh start and, if applicable, resolve old issues. The new organization is being shaped and defined, so take the time to sit back and figure out if there is any way you can make this work in your favor—a new position or a promotion before the new organization completes its staffing. Look around and see what the new situation may offer: a better boss, exciting new challenges, new contacts, and career opportunities. If you perceive the change as an opportunity for a fresh start, a chance to change direction, you can travel through the transition highway with few or no problems at all.

For example, during the time of our company's transition, I took the time to figure out who the decision-makers were, decided where I wanted to be in the new organization, and promoted my skills and brand, making a case for why I was the best person for the job. Fortunately for me, the person offered the job I wanted turned it down, and as runner-up, I got the job. I do not believe this would have been the outcome if I had not taken the time to explore the new organization and promoted my experience, skills, and desires about where I wanted to work.

Manage your perceptions. Stop to examine how you perceive the change and determine whether you are helping or hurting yourself with your perceptions. Focus on letting go of what is familiar by embracing new beginnings. Stop rehashing where you came from and how things were and start getting excited about where you want to go and how you are going to get there.

Be patient. Be patient with yourself and the transitioning from the old to the new. You have made monumental strides and gained a great deal of practical experience and wisdom. All of this learning took time and effort and culminated in the incredible person you are today. Capitalize on all of that experience and put it to work for you in positioning yourself within the new organization.

It is beneficial to view change as necessary for your personal growth. Embrace change and align your words, thoughts, actions, and reactions with your goals, and don't let perceived obstacles distract you. Bask in the wonderment of the possibilities and new territories you will explore and the unique opportunity to reinvent yourself. Determine that this new opportunity will be what you want it to be and aim high. Take your knowledge and experience and build on it to make the most the opportunity the universe has offered.

Change, whether planned or unplanned, imposed or self-imposed, wanted or not, is necessary for your growth. Refrain from making assumptions, jumping to conclusions, and taking the change personally before you have weighed and assessed all the facts. Take it one day at a time and remember that it is your perception of change that affects your thoughts, feelings, actions, and reactions.

Just in case all else fails, fall back on the Serenity Prayer: *"God, grant me the serenity to accept the things I cannot change, the courage to change the things I can, and the wisdom to know the difference."*

> *"If you don't like something, change it. If you can't change it, change your attitude. Don't complain."*
> **Maya Angelou**

CHAPTER 16

POSITIVE DISINTEGRATION

*"Our greatest glory is not in never falling,
but in rising every time we fall."*
Confucius

Positive disintegration is when a major event in your life strikes and swipes away your sense of self. Life as you knew it is gone like the wind. Some people go through these life-altering events and come out the other side stronger and more at peace with themselves, while others fall apart and struggle to carry on. There is no way to predict how any one person will react.

It doesn't have to be a tragedy of massive proportions to spark such a transformation. However, it usually entails the breaking down of a major part of your life. Something that you relied on and cherished as it helped make sense of your world and wore as a badge of honor. The breakdown of this major part of your life sets you on a philosophical journey to find yourself and putting your life back together in line with what you determine to be much more authentic. This event forces you to look inward, grow, and become a better person. You reintegrate your life at a level that is aligned with your inner self. It can take more than a full year to reintegrate your life, and it may result in major changes for you and your family.

Career failure

It is often difficult to pinpoint the exact moment when your career derailed. The deterioration of your career could have been a gradual decline.

Your overconfidence or arrogance could have made you careless about details. Were you too arrogant and obnoxious and the law of cause and effect caught up with you? The law of cause and effect is the law of perfect balance, of logical sequence, and of inevitable consequence. After all, life is a zero-sum game, and life experiences must be in perfect balance. Or it could have happened in one split second, when somebody above you needed a scapegoat, and you were it. Sometimes careers fall apart because life is directing you to move in a different direction.

You did not make it to your current position overnight; it happened over time, with a lot of hard work, late nights, and dedication. Chances are your career derailed the same way, over time, one incident at a time. Regardless of the circumstances, the deterioration of your career can be painful to experience. As you see your life at work falling apart, it soon starts affecting your personal life. Careers should to grow, expand, and flourish, not deteriorate and plummet.

Career failure can be difficult to overcome, and some cannot recover their careers after it has obliterated their ego and self-esteem. Career failure can be a brutally devastating blow that leaves you feeling completely spent and depressed. It is a personal attack on your psyche that cuts way deep down inside, attacking every fiber of your being and soul.

You go through many emotions as you try to figure out what just hit you. You feel afraid and lost, because you cannot seem to identify with that person who has just failed. Going through these emotions is natural, and in order to heal the situation, you must go through every stage of the grieving process, which often includes disbelief, fear, anger, blame, and shame.

The process is unique for every person, and some move through these emotions quickly while others linger an inordinate amount of time on each emotion. You may move back and forth between cycles and back to the beginning, with each iteration lasting less time as you move more quickly through each cycle, until one day it is just a fleeting thought. The key is not to get stuck and move on as quickly as possible. Lingering too long on these negative emotions can impede your progress. Achieving success requires that you not give voice or power to failure. If you want to move forward, try to move through the grieving process as quickly as possible and stop wallowing in self-pity. Whenever you feel trapped in fear or confusion, you are most likely responding to appearances, ego-based fears, and judging a book by its cover. Challenge yourself to dig deeper into the storyline of that book and find the lessons and gifts hidden between the lines.

After you complete the grieving process and humbled into acceptance, you need to have the courage to face the hard truths of your career failure, pick yourself up, and rebuild a more meaningful career on a sturdier foundation. It will require that you to resist the continual urge to ask and try to figure out why this has happened to you. It is human nature to want to know, investigate, and understand what led to the situation. However, you should not waste too much time trying to figure out why something has happened to you. Chances are you may never know the *why*. So, let it go, and move on with your life.

Sometimes failure is the catalyst that provides the kick in the butt or the wake-up call many of us require and offers a fabulous learning opportunity. No one likes to be labeled a failure; however, some of us need to hit rock bottom in order to learn some of the crucial lessons required to succeed.

Failure is not an accident; it results from actions, inactions, and reactions to your environment or situation. It has a definite purpose, structure, and sequence that takes you to greater heights in your life. Take the time to understand your situation so that you can make a plan and take definite action to structure your next move.

Every situation opens a door of opportunity, if we willingly stop long enough to assess the situation and walk through the open door. So, have you truly failed, or is life redirecting your efforts to a more meaningful experience?

What at times appears to be a disaster or failure is life's way of redirecting your path. That challenge or perceived failure brings a valuable life lesson that you may miss if you are caught up in feeling sorry for yourself or lashing out in anger. You need to stop long enough to reflect and capture the lessons that the experience has just delivered, so that you can turn it into success.

Become an advocate for your skills, confidence, and strengths, and not your insecurities and limitations. As a result, you will be more confident and poised and will soar, inspiring others as you empower yourself for that amazing career you deserve.

We all need to borrow a page from Abraham Lincoln's life story. He was a man who knew how to pick himself up, never give up, and is one of the greatest examples of persistence. Abraham Lincoln, the sixteenth president, was defeated for Congress three times, defeated for Senate two times, and defeated for vice president in 1856 before he became president in 1860.

Thomas Edison experimented with thousands of original materials before discovering the filament for the light bulb. When asked how he felt about all of his failures, he denied he had any failures. He stated that he had learned thousands of ways how not to make a light bulb. He persevered to the end. Many times, failure is the first step towards success.

Your past does not define you; your past simply prepares you for future greatness.

My Career Hits a Roadblock

January 2000, I was fortunate to be placed in a business development job responsible for the Latin America portfolio, the job I wanted. But you know what the adage says, "Be careful what you ask for because you just might get it." I failed to recognize the risk of venturing into unfamiliar territory within a new company with new managers. For those of us who took the risk, it meant starting our careers anew. These were people who did not know us at all; in effect, we had no history with the newly merged company.

Within nine months of starting the new job, they reassigned me within the same business development group, from the Latin America portfolio to handle the U.S. portfolio. Maybe I made too much of that re-assignment, but to me, it was like being fired. It devastated me. Nothing like this had ever happened to me, and the worst part of that entire episode was that I never quite knew or understood the why.

It wasn't so much the reassignment. It was the way our management handled it. It was as if they were moving a piece of furniture from one side of the room to the other without stopping to take into consideration the impact on those involved in the shift. Management shrouded the situation in secrecy, with no explanations. Management had decided; case closed.

While managing the Latin America portfolio, I was traveling approximately seventy percent of the time, with a grueling workload. That year was the hardest I had worked in my entire life. I'm not sure how long I could have kept up that routine without affecting my health. Transitioning the business from our affiliates to headquarters was intense. It meant understanding every single aspect of every deal being negotiated. Once I had completed the transition, management handed the portfolio to someone else, and I got zero credit for the grueling work and schedule of the previous nine months. I think it entitled me to a little hostility.

I spent a lot of time trying to understand and figure out where management was coming from. As I went through the classic periods of denial, anger, and depression, I refused to believe that the actions were intentional or malicious. Fortunately, I moved through each of these iterations in a year before I finally accepted the reality of my situation.

From 1982 to 2000, I had made significant strides within the company, promoted ten salary groups in eighteen years. I had broken down the barriers that prevented a secretary from moving up to the contract administration group, the barriers that existed between contract administration and supply operations, the barriers that existed between Supply operations and crude oil trading, and the ones between trading and business development.

I had moved from one professional group to the next, excelling every step of the way. I had that rocket in my pocket. But little did I know I had dropped that rocket somewhere over the Atlantic Ocean sometime between 1999 and 2000. My career went from fantastic to not looking too good to bad to worse, and as my grandson used to say, "the worstest."

I went from being a well known, highly respected professional with a career to an employee whom no one knew with a good-paying job. In effect, they had pulled the ladder out from under me. After eighteen years with the company and having made such significant strides, I had to start over. This was a new beginning. This was another turning point in my career. I was forty-three years old, and not the right time to be starting a career.

This was the job I wanted, but the paternalistic management structure, coupled with the stress of getting a new organization up and running, was fertile ground for misinterpretations and frustrations for all. This was one of the most frustrating environments I've ever had to work in.

I consider myself to be an emotionally strong person. But the management structure coupled with the growing pains of the merged company broke my spirit and my resolve. The domineering, paternalistic, and stifling management style were extremely hard to work with. It stifled my personal, professional, and career growth. I felt as if I were suffocating under the weight of the unnecessary pressure.

The one consolation was that it was not just me who felt this way about working within this structure. There was a consensus; everyone in the group agreed that this management style stifled the creativity of the group with unnecessary stress and undue pressure. Morale was at an all-time low and pressure at an all-time high under this management structure.

On the flip side, I know I did not make life easy for management, as I challenged every misconception that was being attributed to me. This manager had formed an opinion without knowing me as a person or as an employee. No matter what I tried, there was no getting through. Once she had formed an opinion, that was its case closed. Right, wrong, or indifferent, this had sealed my fate with the new company. No amount of hard work and determination will help you get ahead if you do not have a supportive management that believes in you and your abilities.

That year, I ranked at the bottom of our group with no credit for the transitioning of the Latin America portfolio. At that time, I did not put this action into perspective. This job was in the products distribution side of the business, which was totally new territory for me. I had spent the previous eighteen years working in the crude oil side of the industry and knew little about our company's distribution business. All the other folks in the group had some finished products, terminal, or pipeline background. So, in hindsight, being ranked at the bottom that year was not unreasonable. However, I let my ego take it personally.

In the corporate environment, this type of experience is exceedingly difficult to overcome. For all intents and purposes, this was a new company, with new management evaluating my performance. There was nothing I could do or say to influence the outcome. In this person's eyes, my lack of distribution experience disqualified me to be a member of this elite group of people.

Things were so bad under this management structure that I finally decided that it was time for me to move on. I was forty-three years old, in a new company, under new management, and I did not stand a chance. The writing on the wall stated that my career was over. Was this the end of my journey? Is it possible to get back on track after your career derails? These were questions I had no answers to.

Even with those unanswered questions, one thing I had always vowed throughout the years was to be realistic about my career prospects. This new company was offering a job, a well-paying job, but I did not want to kid myself into believing I had a career. I had to reassess my aspirations of moving ahead, because at my level, only a limited few could expect promotions. These were large and competitive rank groups, and any misstep could be detrimental to your career, obliterating any chance of promotion. The higher one goes up in the organization, the fewer the jobs and the tougher the competition.

I embarked on a trip to the world of résumé writing and job hunting to find the answers to my questions. I worked on this process diligently for about a year, and nothing of substance materialized. I read all the relevant articles; I consulted a professional career counselor and signed up with an executive search agency. There were a couple of offers, but none that matched my compensation and benefits package. After a year, I realized that at my age and salary requirement, it would be extremely difficult to move to a new company. I had to face the reality of my situation and resign myself to the fact that I no longer had a career, and for reasons unknown to me, I would remain with this company.

I spent one full year doubting my abilities and worthiness, which was a complete waste of valuable time. Self-pity is a powerful, negative emotion that can hold you hostage and blackmail you emotionally. This mindset did nothing for my personal or professional growth. The intriguing part of this entire situation was that this reaction was totally out of character for me; I had never reacted in this manner before. This was the first time in my adult life that I let anyone break my spirit or let a situation define me as a person.

I felt as if someone had reached deep inside and tried to rip my soul out. But in reality, I was reacting to the devastation and obliteration of my ego and self-esteem, not to the person who was controlling my career, or lack thereof.

I truly believe that nothing happens by accident or by sheer coincidence. All of our relationships play a specific and pivotal role in molding who we are and who we will be in the future. I learned an extremely valuable lesson from my relationship with this manager. I vowed never to let anyone break my spirit and resolve.

I finally stopped fighting my situation and just go with the flow. After a year, humbled into acceptance, and faced the hard truths of my career failure. Destiny was keeping me in this job and this company. I sat back, stopped feeling sorry for myself, and waited to see what destiny had in store for me.

I stopped long enough to reflect on all of my blessings and put my current situation into perspective. I had a lot to be thankful for, and all the blessings outweighed this one devastating experience. I was certainly grateful for everything I had accomplished and the fact that I had a great-paying job with excellent benefits, which was so much more than many could claim.

I put all the negative experiences behind me, where they belonged and where they should stay. I could not let this one experience define who I was as a person or my potential to move forward. So, I shifted the power from the situation that was holding me hostage to viewing my career from an empowered position.

Once I got off the road of self-pity and woe-is-me, I went back to my core values and change my attitude by simply asking what I could learn from this experience. I recognized I had to change my attitude, because it is not productive to harbor two emotions at the same time. Each emotion will determine your mindset and next steps, and there is no way to go simultaneously in two different directions. There was no way I was going to move ahead while feeling like a complete failure.

In order to extract the lesson of what this situation offered, I had to step back and analyze the situation from an empowered vantage point. What did I contribute to this situation? I was too angry to resist the temptation to judge the person and to lash out at the situation with a knee-jerk reaction of hostility. I did not give the situation time to settle, develop, and reveal its true insight and message. I did not take time to understand the bigger picture. I judged the book by its cover, never digging deeper into the storyline and reading between the lines to extract the lesson the situation brought. I let my emotions drive my response, actions, and reactions.

If faced with this same situation today, I would put my ego and pride aside and not internalize or personalize the situation. I would resist the temptation to go into victim mode and become a hostage to my hostility. I would instead try to get down to the why of the decision without wasting too much time rehashing the issue. After all, we shouldn't assume we always know why someone has done something or a certain decision made.

People have their own reasons for doing things, and we can't always jump to the conclusion that it is about us in particular. Often the politics and bureaucracy of a large organization dictate certain actions that may be necessary because of information we are not and never will be privy to, and we simply become collateral damage. There may be a bigger issue that needs to be resolved, and it may require certain actions to ensure its resolution. And most times someone above you needed a scapegoat, and you were it.

I explored what I could learn from this difficult situation. This turned out to be the best strategy for me in coping with the turmoil and upset of my career. I took back control of my career by choosing to make this situation part of my informal education, and I emerged feeling both a sense of honor and responsibility to repair my reputation and career.

Once I changed my mindset and attitude, things changed for me. It wasn't an ideal situation but; we had finally learned to respect and understand each other. There was never a formal apology, and I do not know for sure that the situation warranted one, but the fact that this manager acknowledged my strengths and abilities and added that what had occurred early on was an "unfortunate situation", was good enough for me.

Today, I see this entire situation differently, because I truly believe that some higher power stepped in to redirect my life's journey.

Once I settled down long enough to dig into the storyline, I realized destiny had stepped in to change my path through this experience. For whatever reason, working in the Latin America region was not for me. Early in my career, there were two jobs available, one working with Nigeria and the other with Latin America. Despite my bilingual skills, management assigned me to the West Africa job. The Latin America Business Development Manager job only lasted nine months, just long enough to transition the business to headquarters.

Who knows what fate awaited me with the constant travels to Latin America? I can say that I encountered a couple of disturbing situations when traveling to Latin America. For example, the energy industry is predominantly male dominated, and more so in Latin America where the entire culture is predominantly male dominated. When in negotiations, not once did I ever sit across the table from another woman. The only women I encountered were low-level staff employees, secretaries, or cleaning staff.

On the surface, gender roles and attitudes toward Latin women are straightforward: A woman's place is in the home. Many of the men I encountered did not feel comfortable with my role in representing a major U.S. corporation.

Because I'm of Latin descent, many of the men assumed I knew and understood the Latin culture, and a woman's rightful place. They used my heritage as a license to be disrespectful and make inappropriate comments and sexual innuendos. I have to admit that at first, I was not sure how to handle this behavior. I was not accustomed to being treated this way by my male colleagues in the United States. As a result, I let the comments go the first couple of times. After the third time of inappropriate comments, I realized I had to put an end to this behavior.

During one of our afternoon meetings, my first agenda item was sexual harassment. I opened our meeting with, "Let's get the sexual harassment out of the way so we can have a productive meeting without having to stop for foolish comments, because I am sure that if I were not a Latina, you would not dare behave this way for fear of reprisal." As I looked around the conference room table, waiting for someone to make the first comment, no one said a word. Everyone just kept looking down at their notes. Thankfully, that was the last time I had to deal with the harassments and innuendoes.

One other time, there was a senior person from a Latin America company speculating on how much money the company would pay for my release if I were to be kidnapped. At that time, kidnappings were prevalent in Latin America. I did not think he was kidding. The entire encounter gave me chills and left me feeling very uncomfortable. I'm not sure what would have transpired had I continued traveling to that country.

So, what we perceive as unfair, a roadblock, or failure can actually be a blessing in disguise. Maybe this option is closed to you because destiny has a better option for you or to keep you from harm. So, stop and look around for another open door, and as you walk through, you will understand why the other door closed. The roadblock will disappear, and you can joyfully explore the new path destiny has paved for you.

Unfortunately, my knee jerk reaction and my manager's uninformed assessment had done a lot of damage to my career. It would take a long time and effort to restore and repair the damage from the self-inflicted wounds and the initial unfavorable assessment and evaluation submitted by this manager. I must admit that this manager tried to make up for the "unfortunate situation" and help me by recommending an assignment on a project that had high visibility. I remember not trusting her motives and not even being grateful for the opportunity to showcase my talents. Working on this project was the first step in repairing my reputation and career.

Nothing in life lasts forever, and in the fall of 2001, we received the fantastic news that happy days were here again. Our group was being restructured. This was the best Christmas present I could have ever wished for. I was no longer angry or hostile, but somehow, I knew deep down that a restructuring of our group was probably the best thing that could happen to me. The group was happy and welcomed the new reporting structure. Because of the restructuring, we were reporting directly to the senior manager of the group.

Working directly for the decision-maker of our group was a turning point in lifting the dark cloud that was hanging over me. The first thing I did was ask to have a few minutes of our new manager's time. I asked that he view this as a new start for me. I requested the opportunity to prove what I could bring to the table. It was an open and genuine dialogue, and I was glad that he was receptive.

A year later, during my first performance review, he was extremely complimentary. The words he used were, "I see a vast improvement in your performance." Although flattered, the feedback had taken me aback. People do not change their performance overnight. The quality of my work had not changed. What had changed was my attitude and the fact that I was now working directly for him, without someone else filtering the feedback of my performance. Although tempted to comment, I bit my tongue and decided that it was best just to say, "Thank you," and move on.

The following year, during the second performance review, he was extremely complimentary and had nothing but glowing reports and feedback on my performance. His words touched me in a way that I could not have expected or describe. I was so touched that I had to excuse myself from the conversation, because I was getting too emotional.

He could not understand why I was so emotional. All he said was, "But this is all good. I don't understand."

Once I gathered myself, I went back to finish our conversation and explained to him I did not think I would see the day when I had finally regained my reputation with the company. I also gave him a high level overview of what I had accomplished during the first nine months as the Latin America Business Development Manager, how I had gotten no credit for my accomplishments, and how his recognition on that day was a significant milestone for me. All he said was, "I had no idea."

There are pivotal moments in our lives where the action or words of a person have an immense impact on our lives. This was one of those moments for me. I felt I had finally recovered from that severe blow that had shattered my ego and my self-esteem and left me feeling helpless. I was no longer feeling lost, because now I recognized and could identify with the person he was evaluating. I had regained my sense of self and was no longer mourning the loss of my career. I knew I could now start making plans and hoping for a better and brighter future with the new company.

October 7, 2003, was a new beginning for me. I had regained my confidence and emerged from that dark period a stronger and more confident person. I went through a metamorphosis, during which I shed any insecurities and doubts in my abilities. I emerged feeling equal to everyone around me, even the Ivy League MBA graduates. I felt I was contributing just as much, and sometimes even more than some of the other people.

After three years, I could finally answer my question. It is possible to get back on track after your career has derailed; it just takes some ingenuity, hard work, determination, time, and mentoring.

> *"Success is the ability to go from failure to failure without losing your enthusiasm."*
> **Sir Winston Churchill**

CHAPTER 17

DEVELOP A CAREER PLAN

"A good plan is like a road map: it shows the final destination and usually, the best way to get there."
H. Stanely Judd

Before you embark on the journey of your career, it is imperative that you develop a career plan and a forward looking perspective on your career. Just as you would not embark on a road trip without mapping out the route, you should not embark on your career journey without a plan. Don't just wander along. Make a plan and take control of your career. Following a plan is like following a map. You can always see how much you have progressed towards your goals and how far you have left to reach your destination.

Take charge of your career by developing a career map that puts you in the driver's seat. Having clear direction regarding your career goals and aspirations will minimize your chances of ending up haphazardly moving along a path that does not bring the career satisfaction, reward, and achievement you expected.

Regardless of your career aspirations, it will serve you well to develop a road map, a personal marketing plan to help you along the way. If you are new to your organization or job, settle in and concentrate on mastering your current assignment. However, do not wait too long before you plan your amazing career, which can be long and fruitful if you plan ahead.

You may ask, "why should I make a plan?" Because an effective career road map:

- helps you think through and better understand your objectives
- helps you identify and consider any potential threats or impediments
- helps you plan for the 'what if' and develop a Plan B.
- helps you identify the best route to take to achieve your goals and help you stay on track
- enables you to determine the steps required to develop your skills and expertise
- helps you maximize the opportunities that you will encounter along the way
- allows you to develop strategies that will increase your career satisfaction and success

Developing a plan requires that you invest time and resources. It requires an outside-in thinking approach. What is your environment telling you about your initiative? Look at your plan from an outsider's point of view. Developing your plan also requires that you be open-minded, letting go of entrenched thinking.

Think strategically about your vision for the future. Identify your goals and objectives for your initiatives and establish a timeline for when to implement your goals. Strategic planning is not limited to large corporations, as it can help you succeed in business and prosper in your career and personal endeavors. You can take control of your future endeavor's by developing a strategic plan.

The strategic plan involves listing a mission statement as well as clearly documenting business goals. It requires that you look at outside of your environment to see what is the best approach to enhance your situation. It helps you plan for the "What if" scenarios by considering what's happening around you that will impact your initiative. Determine your vision and identify your goals and objectives. Establish the sequence in which your goals should be implemented. Develop action items, a Plan B, and a clear mission, goals, and objectives.

Develop a three—or five-year plan. An effective plan should include detailed action steps and target completion dates. As you reach each milestone, celebrate your success, take a moment to rest, and then update your plan for the next three years. When updating your plan, include all the new things that you have discovered along the way. Also, take a moment to look back and reassess the road you have just traveled, as it will help you map the route that will lead you to the next plateau.

Make your plan a living document and be flexible and open to potential changes. Review your plan every year to see if it requires tweaking or development of an alternate route. There may be some circumstances that you had not anticipated which may require a change in direction. Make this a living document and be flexible and open to potential changes.

In addition to this career GPS (global positioning system), your plan will help you manage your time and resources. Few people take the time to develop a formal plan. Having a plan will distinguish you from your peers and the competition. Develop a plan around your innate strengths and abilities, and you will discover your genuine passion.

Developing your career plan

Below, I have outlined some things that you may want to consider when developing and planning your career. I do not intend this to be all-inclusive, and one size certainly does not fit all. So, take what works for you, and leave the rest behind.

Define your personal purpose, vision, and mission statements. Define your purpose statement and develop a personal career mission and vision statement. Vision and mission statements are very similar, but have different purposes.

- Your purpose statement defines the why and goes beyond your job and defining goals. It includes everything in your career. It is your definition of success. It includes short—and long-term goals for where you want to be in the future. Your purpose can also encompass your passion, your life's mission, your reason for being. Identifying your purpose takes time and commitment.

- Your **vision** statement defines the *what* of your accomplishment. It is your aspirational destination. It describes what you want to achieve in the future; helps to provide a focus for your mission. It answers the question "Where do I want to be?" It defines the optimal desired future state—the mental picture. It inspires you to give your best and shapes your understanding of what you want to accomplish.

- Your **mission** follows the path you chart to arrive at your destination, it is the *how*. Your mission drives your chosen path. It describes what you want now and how you will achieve it. It spells out overall goals, provides a sense of direction: What do I do?", "How do I do it?", "Who do I do it for?", "What makes me different, and "What is the benefit? It is the present leading to the future, and how you will get there.

Develop a brand. What is going to be your professional brand? What do you want your legacy to be? Self-branding does not differ from the branding and marketing of a product. In order for a product to sell and be successful in the market, it has to have an excellent reputation and brand recognition. Self-branding is about discovering and figuring out what you want to do for the rest of your life. It is about setting goals, writing a career mission, vision and personal brand statement, and creating a development plan that is aligned with your personal purpose statement. Developing a brand and a marketing strategy will help you discover your abilities, strengths, and that distinctive element that makes you unique and marketable.

Ground Zero. Identify your starting point. Develop a Strength, Weaknesses, Opportunities, and Threats (SWOT) analysis. You must be brutally honest with yourself regarding your current situation, where and how far you want to go or believe you can go, and how, who, or what can help you get to where you want to go. When identifying your ground zero, it is imperative that you fully understand and recognize your management's assessment of your potential and career path so you can realistically determine the time it will take to reach your goals. Consider this a mission, and as with any mission, you need to state exactly what it is you want to accomplish and how you are going to accomplish it.

Goals. Set long and short-term goals. Short-term goals can be 90, 120, or 365 days. Your long-term goals should be where you see yourself within your company or industry in the next three to five years and how you are going to get there. These goals should be specific and measurable. Directly align your goals with your career development plans with those your management envisions for you. Goal setting is critical to managing your strategies. It is the single most important life skill that very few people develop. You can use goal setting in every single area of your life.

- **Germane**–Relevant: Before you even set goals, it's a good idea to sit down and define your core values and your life purpose because they will ultimately decide how and what goals you choose for your life. Goals, in and of themselves, do not provide happiness or success.
- Goals that are in harmony with our life purpose do have the power to help us reach our highest potential.
- **Obtainable**–Achievable: Setting big goals is great, but setting unrealistic goals will just de-motivate you. A good goal is one that challenges, but is not so unrealistic that you have virtually no chance of accomplishing it.
- **Assessable**–Measurable: It's crucial for goal achievement that you can track your progress towards your goal. That's why all goals need an objective measuring system so that you can stay on track and become motivated when you enjoy the sweet taste of quantifiable progress.
- **Limited**–Timed: Without setting deadlines for your goals, you have no compelling reason or motivation to work on them. By setting a deadline, your subconscious mind works on that goal, night and day, to bring you closer to achievement.
- **Specific**–In order for you to achieve a goal, you must be clear about what you want. Create a list of the benefits that the accomplishment of your goal will bring to your life. Review that

list regularly so you can remind yourself of the good that is awaiting.

Actions. Identify any required changes, improvements, or actions that you need to address in order to achieve your career goals and how you plan to close those gaps. These should include any actions that capitalize on your strengths, skills, and experience. List the required actions in chronological order and assign each action step a target completion date. Your plan should include actions you will need to help you master your current assignment and help propel you to that next plateau. For example, do you need to work on your leadership skills? How are your oral and written communication skills? Are there any deficiencies you need to work on improving?

Target job assignment. Identify a position or job you would like to be considered for and prepare a marketing campaign for that product called *You*. Why are you the best person for this job? What do you bring to the table that will benefit the corporation? Do you possess a skill that may give you a competitive edge? Are you bilingual, do you have exceptional skills in technology, spreadsheets, or other valuable skills that distinguish you from the competition?

Roadblocks. Anticipate any potential roadblocks and develop a strategy to help you overcome some of those barriers. For example, is your current supervisor supportive of your plans, or is he perceived to be a roadblock? If you perceive your immediate supervisor to be a roadblock, then you need to identify and address the issue as soon as possible. No amount of hard work and determination will help you get ahead if you do not have a supportive management that believes in you and your abilities.

Resources. Identify the resources available to assist you in achieving your career plans. These resources might include, but are not limited to, key people with specific expertise, training courses, networking, your boss, Human Resources, colleagues, working on a high-visibility project, or employee resource group within your company that can help you enhance your leadership skills and confidence.

Engage Mentors. Get several mentors who can help you achieve and meet your plan. Strive for a balance of male and female mentors, because there will be times when you will need advice from both. Think of a mentor as your career GPS. Your mentor will guide you on your career journey, providing guidance and direction.

Network. Give your brand the required visibility to get an excellent reputation by networking with your coworkers and other professionals within your field. Get to know people so that people can get to know you. If you learn the art of leveraging your personal style, values, and talents, and mastering the art of self-promotion, you can attain the success you deserve.

As you develop your plan, remember that your career requires that you take a holistic approach. It requires well-rounded experiences and education, always understanding and abiding by those unwritten rules and regulations of your work environment.

Stop, think, and reflect on what you can do to help progress your career.

Don't over-plan – take action

Some people make plans set goals, but never seem to execute the plan. They get so caught up with the planning that they fail to take action, which is another form of procrastination.

Better to take action and execute your plan and update your plan as you go along. Stay on top of changes in your environment and adjust your plan as necessary. There should be continuous re-evaluation of your plan.

You can sit back and wait for your career to happen. But in order to achieve the results you really want, then you need to be proactive and develop a career plan for your personal growth and career success. As you develop and then execute your plan, remember that your career requires that you take a holistic approach. It requires well-rounded experiences and education, always understanding and abiding by those unwritten rules and regulations of your work environment.

> *"If you don't know where you are going, you'll end up someplace else."*
> **Yogi Berra**

PART III

WOMEN IN THE WORKPLACE

CHAPTER 18

MAKE EQUALITY A REALITY

"No country can ever truly flourish if it stifles the potential of its women and deprives itself of the contribution of half its citizens."
Michelle Obama

Women have come a long way but continue to have a long way to go before they achieve gender parity. Many women continue to face obstacles and barriers that hinder their ability to climb the corporate ladder and achieve the recognition they deserve.

In some industries, women still grapple with and bump up against the proverbial glass ceiling that says, "You can advance just this far but no further." Unfortunately, no matter how hard some women have tried over the years, they have not shattered and removed that glass ceiling. Those women who have broken through the glass ceiling could do so because they set high standards for themselves. Hillary Clinton could not "shatter that highest, hardest glass ceiling but left it with ~66 million cracks" in 2016.

There are certainly many more women in the energy industry today than when I started in 1982. But in 2017, at the end of my career, I still looked around the conference room table and, more often than not, I was still the only woman.

Corporate America has made significant strides; however, it will take more time for the environment to become more women friendly.

Because no matter how smart, talented, or successful a woman is, there is still the cultural difference that separates men and women.

Early in life, we learn that there are innate physical differences between men and women and although both have many things in common, society has created the male and female classification which we used to classify both ourselves and others. Historically, the differences between men and women have been socially defined by the male perspective, which assumed that men were superior.

As we strive for equality between the sexes, we must be careful not to lose the importance of our differences when trying to be politically correct. It is essential that we recognize both the similarities and differences between men and women. Men and women are equal and should be treated equally for rights and opportunities. However, men and women are different for the obvious physical attributes and the less obvious psychological. The psychological differences can influence our view of the world and how we develop and nurture our personal and business relationships.

Organizations should consider women equal to men, yet also value the fresh perspective they bring to the workplace. Women need to recognize how these differences affect decisions within their own environment and learn how to maximize and use their innate abilities.

Claiming that you are bumping up against the glass ceiling implies the corporation is not supportive of advancing women, and this may or may not be the case. Before claiming that you are bumping up against the 'glass ceiling', you should first take a long, hard look at your circumstance. Evaluate your current situation and make an honest assessment about what may hinder your progress.

- Is it education or a specific skill that needs developing and perfecting? Depending on the job, is an MBA or other advanced degree required?
- Have you developed a network?
- Have you identified your brand and developed a marketing plan for that product called *You*?
- How are your communication skills?
- When was the last time you showcased your talents by volunteering to lead a work team or other work-related event?

- Have you developed a career plan outlining your goals and aspirations and how you will reach those goals?
- Stop, think, and reflect on what you can do to help progress your career.

2018 ushered in a major shift in women's perception and acceptance with the 'Me Too' and 'Times Up' movements striving to make "equality a reality". Women have reached the tipping point and are feeling empowered to speak up — "No M**ás**" — "We are not going to take it anymore".

The various movements took down many powerful men in various industries who had been molesting women for decades. These men abused the power of their positions to intimidate and molest. Women are finally holding these men accountable for their reprehensible behavior and actions.

Women have come a long way since the 'bra burning' days of the 60s when they started protesting for equal rights and looking to reform the stereotype that recognized women as housewives and mothers only. Despite the advances of the last 50+ years, women continue to have a long way to go before they achieve gender parity. Many women continue to face obstacles and barriers that hinder their ability to excel in their given professions and achieve the recognition they deserve.

All over the world, women continue to experience the lack of equality with fewer opportunities for basic and higher education. But the fight for women's equality is in the forefront of movements like 'Women's Equality Party', 'She Should Run', 'UN Women', and 'Equality Now' as they work to ensure that women around the world get equal rights, get protection from domestic and sexual abuse, and are provided with adequate education.

> *"We have to be careful in this era of radical feminism, not to emphasize an equality of the sexes that leads women to imitate men to prove their equality. To be equal does not mean you have to be the same."*
> **Eva Burrows**

CHAPTER 19

THE FEMALE LEADERSHIP CONUNDRUM

"Any woman who understands the problems of running a home will be nearer to understanding the problems of running a country."
Margaret Thatcher

As a culture, we are still condemning women who are too aggressive or assert their right to power, even though these are the precise traits associated with effective leaders. This negative connotation puts women in leadership positions in a double bind, as they face the formidable task of balancing authority without being autocratic.

If a woman chooses assertiveness and forcefulness, we perceive her to be a 'bitch.' If she exhibits too much compassion, then she doesn't have what it takes to handle a powerful leadership position. Power can be a tough balancing act for some women, but the key is to be assertive without the fear of being labeled a 'bitch'.

Many women are still taking a back seat and not claiming their right to the driver's seat for their leadership style, and too often struggle with power and control at work. Women should be assertive and stand up for their right to take the driver's seat by coming out of the shadows and making themselves visible to their management and peers; exhibit their personal power and charisma by speaking up for themselves with confidence without compromising their values. Women must fully develop their communication skills so that they can communicate in a direct, concise, and compelling fashion.

At home, many women are CEOs (Chief Executive Officer) and CFOs (Chief Financial Officers) of their families. They successfully lead their families, church groups, plan many social and charity events, and succeed in many other leadership roles in the home and social fronts. As mothers and wives, they have practiced and perfected their leadership skills, which most times are transferable to the workplace.

Rearing a family, managing the day-to-day of running a home, or planning events is not exactly the same as leading a work group. However, many of the skills required to lead a staff, project, or work team are the same as those required when running a home and raising children. As CEO and CFO of their families, women manage and resolve issues that enhance their leadership skills and performance; for example, women:

- deal with and mediate difficult situations with spouse,
- children, and in-laws
- multitask, delegate, and collaborate with the rest of the family
- organizational skills are necessary in order to ensure that all tasks get completed on time
- prepare and negotiate schedules with other parents, sitters, and many other day-to-day activities and appointments
- negotiate with contractors and oversee home-improvement and construction projects.
- develop budgets for their family's day-to-day, vacations, future expenses, and retirements
- teach their children about values and ethical behavior

The above is the tip of the iceberg on the activities that require leadership skills. There are hundreds of examples of daily tasks performed by women that hone their leadership skills. I'm sure that you can come up with a few yourself.

Every woman will develop a unique combination of skills depending on their family structure. The bottom line is that these skills are transferable to the workplace. Stop and think about all the skills you have developed and perfected over the years in your day-to-day activities as CEO and CFO of your family. How can you transfer those same skills to your workplace with the same confidence and effectiveness? Women can confidently showcase their power by openly displaying their knowledge, skills, and being prepared when addressing management, peers, and competitors. This way management and their peers will judge them as individuals with exceptional ideas that can positively impact the organization.

The key is to learn how to exert power and leadership skills in a manner that helps others and enhances your self-esteem and self-worth. Do not to let your work environment intimidate you. You must believe in your strengths and abilities and cast out all doubt from your mind. Develop an authentic, personal style you feel comfortable with so you can showcase your talents and boost your confidence.

Experts agree that the ideal leadership teams should comprise a balance of men and women with their differing traits, management styles, risk profile, and collaboration. They also agree that the female brain and creativity can positively impact the bottom line. Today, there are many more women in the corporate environment, and many men do not know how to handle their creativity and unique way of problem-solving.

Eleanor Roosevelt's observation that "a home requires all the tact and all the executive ability required in any business" is supported by two surveys. *Wellesley College Center for Research on Women and the Center for Creative Leadership in Greensboro, North Carolina* conducted individual surveys of approximately one hundred twenty (sixty in each group) successful female managers. These surveys confirmed that parenting teaches transferable skills and that multiple life roles enhanced their professional leadership performance. The surveys also found that most of the participants who had children thought that being a mother had made them better executives and had been an excellent training ground for developing their leadership skills.

However, when having to display these same leadership qualities at work, many women are afraid of exerting their power and style. They are afraid of taking a leadership position, feeling unsure of their ability to lead and the perception of their peers. Some women feel intimidated by the extroverts and bullies in their work environment. As a result, they become invisible, not speaking up or giving themselves credit for all the experience they have gained over the years.

The University of California-Irvine professor emeritus Judy Rosener reports that brain scans prove that male and female brains operate differently. Rosener concluded that a company with a leadership team that comprised male and female will outperform a company that relies on the leadership of a single sex. Rosener also concluded that women aren't better, but they bring to the table something that men don't have and that a company dominated by women would not outperform a company dominated by men. (Judy Rosener cited in "Women slowly gain on Corporate America" by Del Jones in *USA Today* January 2, 2009)

Sandra Witelson, a neuroscientist, agrees with the differences in male and female brains, stating, "There are clear differences in the brain between men and women, both in structure and chemistry, which includes hormones and neurotransmitters and what's connected to what." Some studies show that, because of brain "structure and wiring," men use only one side of the brain to process some problems, while women employ both sides (*Why Are There Differences in Gender Behavior? March 2010*).

Similar studies have concluded that there are differences in the brains of adult men and women. However, these differences result from life experiences and the different treatment boys and girls receive while growing up. These studies imply brains can change their structure and function in response to the environment. (*Why Are There Differences in Gender Behavior? March 2011*)

Other studies support the notion that biology and upbringing have a lot to do with the differences between the genders. That gender differences come from nature and nurture. These differences in the cultural roots of men and women are also the roots of a gentler style of leadership skills.

Some research shows that women have a *transformational* leadership style and men are more *transactional*. This means that most women who adopt the transformational style are not only interested in getting the deal done; they are also interested in a collaborative, relationship building approach.

So, is it nature, nurture, or a combination of the two? The answer to which of these theories is correct is still being debated. However, as mothers, daughters, wives, aunts, and sisters, women are relationship-builders, collaborative in their approach and intuitive by nature. Because women wear so many hats, they develop a variety of skills that enhance their management perspective and leadership styles, which makes them valuable members of any executive leadership team.

If women continue to take a back seat, they will never achieve gender parity in the workplace. Women have to learn to take charge of their careers and their rightful place in the workplace, as this is the only way they will achieve the recognition they deserve.

"Whenever you see a successful woman, look out for three men who are going out of their way to try to block her."
Yulia Tymoshenko

CHAPTER 20

MANAGING PERSONAL CONTROVERSY

*"Professional is not a label you give yourself,
it's a description you hope others will apply to you."*
David Maister

Just as in life, there are some controversial issues that arise in the workplace that are difficult to manage. Some are organizational while others are personal. Strive to stay focused on your professional goals and trying to improve yourself, your career, and your work relations with other team members.

Unfortunately, when competing in the corporate environment, some women can at times be their own worst enemies. Their own actions and behaviors can be one of the primary reasons women cannot get ahead in the corporate environment.

Sometimes, women overtly display jealousy toward their successful peers. This inability to control their emotions and exhibit a professional demeanor can sometimes be career-limiting.

As women, we need to learn how to manage controversy and competition in a more effective and professional manner. Some spend too much time gossiping, backstabbing, and displaying inappropriate dramatic behavior. This is not only unprofessional, but it detracts their ability to get ahead. Women need to stop taking work related disagreements personally. Ten years later, women will still bring up the same disagreement. Ladies, we need to learn how to compartmentalize and let go.

So where do women learn these obnoxious behaviors? What do men learn as they grow up those women are not privy to? Is it their prevalence to take part in organized sports, where they are fierce competitors on the field and then socialize after the event? I don't know the answer to these questions. What I do know is that, as women, we are picking up some of these reprehensible behaviors from the female role models in our lives.

These detestable behaviors do not help us in the corporate world. In fact, they are at the top of the list of why some women do not get ahead in corporate America. If women want to move the needle that measures gender parity, they need to behave differently, so that they can be better role models and teach the young ladies in the pipeline how to be professional competitors, win, lose, or draw.

Men compete for assignments and disagree on issues at work and at the end of the discussion, they go to lunch, play golf, and mostly support each other. They either don't take it personal or can mask their feelings. They move on and develop long-lasting relationships, which translates into developing that next male executive.

Early in my career, I worked in a group that was primarily women from the top down. This group was drama central. This type of environment can be like a three-ring circus, with all the drama, distractions, gossiping, backstabbing, and inappropriate dramatic vindictive behavior. Mostly, the behavior was unprofessional when working with someone they did not like, with most often falling victim to their own inability to remain objective while at work.

Unfortunately, twenty-five years later, this same group was still primarily women and still facing the same issues and still perceived as not being sufficiently professional. Women caught up in this behavior allow the rivalries—real or perceived—to cloud their judgment.

Managing the green monster

One of the primary personal issues that many contend with in the workplace is envy. Envy is a powerful emotion that threatens personal relationships, career advancement, and the cohesiveness of the work team. Envy can drive some people to misbehave and nobody wins. If you find yourself facing the green monster, below are some recommended strategies.

Separate yourself from the drama. Do your best to separate yourself from the drama, and just do your job; it will pay off in the long run. Do not let yourself get distracted by the surrounding drama, as it will knock you off of your professional track. Stay focused on your priorities so you can achieve your goals and objectives. Separating yourself from the distractions of the daily drama may not make you popular with your peers, but it will be much better for your career.

Change your attitude. Adopt a "what you think about me is none of my business" attitude – worry less about what jealous teammates think. Be more concerned with what those managing your career think.

Understanding the issue. If you want to resolve the issue with your coworker, try to identify where the negative feelings are coming from. Is the person threatened by you and your abilities and perceives you as a threat to their career? Whether your coworkers' feelings are real or perceived, try to reach out to the person. Being direct in a civil and professional manner about the situation in a public setting may allow your coworker to address the issue and move on.

Maintain your professionalism. If it is somebody you equally detest or envy, try to keep a professional demeanor at work. Avoid interactions with the person. If you must work together, be pleasant and treat the person with respect.

Be honest with yourself. Identify what makes you envious of this person and try to address the issue. If you are envious of a coworker's promotion, you need to accept the fact that we all have hidden mixed feelings about another's success. Be professional and congratulate your coworker on their promotion. Remember, you can't win them all. Find another opportunity within or outside of the company that you can target.

Don't compare yourself. Stop focusing and comparing yourself to others–focus on yourself. Instead of comparing yourself to others, you should make a list of your recent accomplishments. Honestly reassess your skills, experience, and potential. Address any skill gap to better position you for that next promotion. When you constantly compare yourself to others, it can lead to feelings of envy.

When you feel threatened or find yourself envious of another, remind yourself of your strengths and past successes. Positive reinforcement can go a long way towards easing the intensity of potential envy. Your coworkers' success does not diminish your chances of a successful career.

> *"Envy is the art of counting the other fellow's blessings instead of your own.*
> **– Harold Coffin.**

Keeping women in the pipeline

Having qualified people in top jobs—or any job—should be the goal of any employer. However, female role models in leadership positions should focus on ensuring that the young women in the pipeline get the proper training, education, and empowerment that will permit them to position themselves for that next promotion, regardless of the assignment.

When you look around, you see women choosing and succeeding in careers, in many fields. So, you would surmise that now that women are succeeding, they would have developed a solid support system to ensure that the pipeline of successful women continues to flow. And to some extent, they have, so long as they do not perceive the woman they are supporting as a threat. As women move up through the corporate ranks, they often leave in their wake peers who are not happy for them and instead exhibit jealousy, envy, or resentment. I have experienced the overt resentment towards me when management announced that I was being promoted. There were no congratulations forthcoming from the women in our group.

The corporate arena can be extremely competitive, a survival-of-the-fittest environment. More often than not, underneath the sweetness and words of encouragement, there is a shark lying in wait, ready to rip you apart or set you up for failure. Unfortunately, it is extremely difficult to identify such a person, because they are extremely masterful at hiding their devious side. As a result, it's difficult to prove their depths of deception to anyone else, especially senior management. These women never exhibit their true colors in front of their bosses, and their so-called professionalism, poise, confidence, and intelligence often dupes senior management. Sadly, some of these women are on a mission to destroy your hopes and dreams. This is not to imply that some men do not behave in this manner because they do. However, since men are in most of the executive ranks, they are less likely to see a female colleague as a threat.

The higher women move up in the corporation, the uglier the behavior and fiercer the competition. This behavior is likely fueled by the fact that there are fewer jobs at the top of the pyramid, and each wants to be the one to get that next promotion. Not only are they competing with other women, but they are also competing with their male counterparts.

A 2008 study, part of behavioral scientist Shannon L. Goodson's book, *The Psychology of Sales Call Reluctance,* compared to approximately 11,500 professional females with approximately 16,700 males from around the world. The study concluded that women can at times be their own worst enemies when climbing the corporate ladder. This international study found that women are less likely to promote themselves and network than their male counterparts. "Women did not create the glass ceiling, the invisible barrier blamed for limiting their ability to earn what they're worth, but they help maintain it," Goodson wrote.

A portion of Goodson's research conducted primarily in the U.S. shows that many female executives are not as supportive or as encouraging of female staff, and sometimes sabotage the chances of other female workers seeking promotion. The study also found that these female executives tended to 'take the ladder with them,' once they reached the top. "This led many women in the study to actually prefer male managers to female managers, claiming men are more consistent and fair-minded than women," Goodson added.

Many women in senior management positions often refuse to get involved and help promote and support other women. It is sad that the women we should look up to as role models are the ones exhibiting the least professional and most obnoxious behavior. These women abuse their power. They do not use their power to help other women in the pipeline.

My thirty-four-year corporate career was in a male dominated industry. During that time, some had admitted to me they were afraid of some women in the corporate environment. Not because they are powerful, smart, or successful, but because some women were too sensitive and sometimes could not control their emotions. They too had encountered that shark lying in wait to rip apart anyone that impedes their path to the top of the organization. So, what happens? John decides he will play it safe and take Joe instead of Jane under his wing for development and advancement.

Ladies, be realistic about your personal situation. Are there really gender issues in your environment, or is there some skill set that you are lacking or some behavior pattern that requires modification?

"It's possible to climb to the top without stomping on other people."
Taylor Swift

CHAPTER 21

CAREER, FAMILY, OR BOTH?

"Never get so busy making a living that you forget to make a life."
Dolly Parton

Gender issues are not only about the glass ceiling. They are also about the delicate balancing of work and personal lives. Fortunately, many companies recognize that taking care of family matters and raising children aren't just women's issues—they are family issues.

Many women feel torn by having to choose between having a family and their careers and earnestly answer the question: Am I prepared to make the sacrifices that are required in order to break through the glass ceiling? More often than not, the answer is a resounding, "No, my family comes first."

Responsibility to family, childcare in particular, is one of the primary reasons women leave the workforce, and this makes it challenging to have a critical mass for quantifying women in the professional work environment.

Some believe that choosing to pursue motherhood and a career sub-optimizes both and opt for one. Some of the most successful women in our corporate environment have made a conscious decision not to have children and instead dedicated one hundred percent of their time and energy to their careers.

Choosing between work and family is a highly personal decision that takes many circumstances into consideration, and only you and your family can make the final decision. Decide and be happy with your choice whether you want to be a stay-at-home mom, be a working mom, or be childless and dedicate your life to your career.

The luxury of choice

It is a fact of life that many women do not have the luxury of choice. Today, women represent approximately fifty percent of the workforce, and two-thirds of women in the workforce are the primary breadwinner or co-breadwinner of their families. Some of the most common positions held by women (administrative assistants, nurses, teachers, first-line supervisors, and receptionists) are not highly paid jobs. There is absolutely nothing wrong with these professions, but what is wrong is that women who hold these positions are still making less than their white male counterpart's income and much less if they are African American or Latina.

I've often wondered why women get paid less money than men for the same job. I suspect it could be because of the outdated paternalistic cultural, social model that puts the man at the head of the family. Wake up America, the family structure has changed dramatically since the 50s, when most women were homemakers and those who worked were doing so in order to supplement the primary breadwinner's salary or have their own spending money. There is no longer just one model for the traditional family. In some minority cultures, women outnumber men in being the primary breadwinner for their families. And yet, minority women are the ones paid the least for their work, which forces them to take on a second job. African American women and Latinas are carrying the burden of having to raise a family on much less than the balance of the population.

There are those that don't have to, but choose to, be working mothers. Many women who choose to be working mothers do so for various reasons. They want to have their own money, continue to advance their careers, maintain their independence, or keep their identity, to name a few.

Regardless of the reason a woman opts to be a working mom, the guilt of leaving the children in the care of others is often a serious factor in her peace of mind. She often feels conflicted about where her schedule requires her to be versus where she would prefer to be. In fact, approximately fifty percent of working moms feel guilty at least once a day. The key for working mothers is to manage the feelings of guilt. Guilt is a negative emotion that may hinder a working mom's ability to make effective decisions, which can cause her to fail both at work and at home.

It is difficult to concentrate on work if you do not have reliable childcare. A trustworthy childcare provider helps working parents financially and emotionally. Knowing that you have a person who you can trust with your children without worrying about their well-being is priceless.

Reliable childcare

Having reliable daycare helped me accomplish my educational and career goals. I could not have done it without the help of my husband and the woman who became our sitter, grandmother, and mother during the years my children required at home care.

Fortunately, my husband was way ahead of his time by being the only Mr. Mom I knew. During the early to mid '80s, being a Mr. Mom was not common, and taking care of children was a woman's job, especially within our Latino community. He took on some of the duties and responsibilities of the day-to-day care of our family.

I achieved my career and educational goals with my husband's help, an excellent sitter, and Pace, a university that met the needs of working students.

My husband and I had a balanced distribution of responsibilities in the home. For example, depending on our schedules, whoever came home first would make dinner, while the other picked up the boys from a sporting event. We capitalized on each other's strengths and expertise in dividing up the responsibilities on the home front.

The bottom line is that all the responsibility for taking care of the children and home should not rest with the woman, especially if she is a working mother.

Every family is unique

Whether you work full time or part time, finding the balance between your career and your family is crucial. Many parents struggle to find the right balance between their careers and nurturing their relationship with their children.

There is no single solution to balancing both worlds. Each family's situation is as unique as each of its members. Your family's health, economic condition, extended family, and resources at your disposal as a parent will dictate the best solution for you. The key is to stay true to yourself, your goals, and your family.

While it is hard to break the glass ceiling, it's even harder when you are raising children. Women wear many more hats than men as caregivers, nurturer, and home keepers. As a result, women have to take off more time from work than men to resolve family issues.

When women are formulating their plans on how best to balance their career and family, they should also include a balancing of duties on the home front. Sometimes, the family needs a redistribution of duties between women and their significant others to balance the duties. This balancing of duties can go a long way in helping a woman succeed in her career and her family as a mother and wife.

Depending on the choices you make, you can certainly limit or even end your career. The fact of the matter is that someone has to be available to take care of the children and the home, whether it is the man or woman.

Young women in the workforce need to understand that they do not have to be stay-at-home moms in order to be excellent mothers. They can be excellent mothers and still have a successful career. It does not have to be one or the other. They can do both. It just takes a little more time management, organization, patience, and ingenuity.

The essential thing is to be true to yourself with the goal of balancing and integrating both worlds successfully, if you choose. In doing so, remember to take care of yourself first. Too many women are so focused on taking care of family members and work responsibilities that they forget about their own personal needs. The safety message on the airplane tells you to put your oxygen mask on first before helping the person seated next to you; this philosophy also applies on the ground within your family.

> *"You will never feel truly satisfied by work until you are satisfied by life."*
> **Heather Schuck**

PART IV

EMPOWER YOURSELF FOR AN AMAZING CAREER

CHAPTER 22

PERSONAL EMPOWERMENT – WHY IT MATTERS.

"Nobody can make you feel inferior without your consent."
Eleanor Roosevelt

Are you in control of your life, your career? Is your life what you imagined it would be? Or have you somehow allowed yourself to be deterred from your chosen path? Did you know that nothing changes unless you change it?

No matter what you seek, it can only happen if you do something about it. Take charge of your personal power. To be empowered, you must know what you want for your life and why. What do you really want? Be clear on what you want and you will get it quicker than if you harbor mixed feelings or take action based on trying to please others.

What is personal empowerment?

Personal empowerment is a collection of beliefs, actions and skills all working together to help you achieve your goals and begins with two things: self-awareness and a positive mindset.

- Self-awareness. You need to know your strengths and weaknesses. The awareness that's required doesn't stop with your skills and abilities. It also includes your values and your goals. Self-awareness of your strengths and weaknesses—skills and abilities plus your values and goals is a must. This is your ground zero. Identifying your unique and transferable skills and strengths will help you define and refine your personal brand so that you can enhance your marketability.

- A positive mindset. It's important to have a positive but realistic view of yourself. A positive but realistic view of yourself will go a long way to help you achieve your goals. It's not enough to want to achieve a goal; you must know and believe that you can achieve your goal. Believe in yourself, your abilities, and your judgment. When you believe you can change things or make a difference in a situation, you are much more likely to succeed. If you think you can't, you won't. It becomes a self-fulling prophecy. You must be ready, willing and able to go after what you want. If you don't follow through and take action, nothing happens and you can get stuck in a never-ending loop of setting goals, planning and learning for years.

Personal empowerment comes down to belief in yourself and follow-through. Be presumptuous enough to believe that you are just as good as, as smart as, or better than those around you and that you have a significant contribution to make.

Break free of the power you have given others over your life, as you will ultimately have to live with the outcome of the choices you make. Free yourself of self-doubt, negativity, and people that do not have a positive influence in your life.

Nothing in your life will change unless you change it. Whether you seek money, marriage, or a career, it will only happen if you do something about it. The only way to live the life you imagined for yourself is to empower yourself to direct and take control of your life. The bottom line is that it is up to you to take the steps necessary to make change happen. Take the unique skills and talents you have to offer and make what you want out of it, whether it is a certain career, personal endeavor, retirement, new house, or other goal.

Personal empowerment is a collection of beliefs, actions and skills all working together to help you achieve your goals, and it begins with two things: self-awareness and a positive mindset. No matter what you seek, it can only happen if you do something about it. Take charge of your personal power.

You can live your life or your life can live you. Take control of your life and your life will be what you imagined it would and could be. However, if you let your life live you, you'll continue to be a victim of circumstance and continue to live a life that isn't aligned with your goals.

> *"Believe in yourself and all that you are. Know that there is something inside you greater than any obstacle."*
> **Christian D. Larson**

CHAPTER 23

EXPRESS YOUR TRUTH

"Today you are You, that is truer than true.
There is no one alive who is Youer than You."
Dr. Seuss

Are you displaying the authentic *You* to the world? You are an individual, and there is no one else exactly like you. Your personal attributes are the things that distinguish and set you apart from your competition. So leverage your personal style, values, and talents, and don't be shy about self-promoting them.

Self-expression is the key ingredient to reaching your full potential. When you live true to yourself, you avoid becoming frustrated and depressed. Bottling up your true self may result in a loss of your identify and cause you to become exasperated, frustrated, and depressed as you lose your sense of self. Expressing the truth about the real you can help you get back on track and avoid losing your self-identity.

Most of what you think about yourself is learned from outside opinions. You have adopted dark self-images that have been projected onto you by others who do not know or love themselves. Unfortunately, whether intentional or unintentional, some relationships shape and ingrain a negative reflection of self into our consciousness through years of disappointments, uncertainties, and doubt. These negative reflections stay with us and develop our overall impression of ourselves and life, limiting our experiences to what our ego-based fears allow.

The ego is shallow and fear-based, and its primary focus is all about 'me.' With this kind of focus, you are bound to fail, making your worst fears come true. Ego-based fears can be powerful and control our minds. If our self-image is threatened, the ego diligently goes to work by partnering with fear, creating a cycle of fearful thoughts, perceptions, and ideas.

The ego's role is to help you clearly understand your personal needs, values, and goals in life. It is constantly reminding us who we should be by evaluating and manipulating fear-based emotions, such as inadequacy, humiliation, and failure. These fear-based emotions can drown you in pool of your own negativity, as your mind reminds you repeatedly of your weaknesses, powerlessness, and hopelessness. It is destructive to indulge in self-pitying thoughts and emotions, so take the time to identify and heal all insecurities. Stop being your own worst enemy and harshest critic.

When you feel worthless and powerless, you sometimes begin to attract circumstances, relationships, and situations that affirm that belief. Your body language will manifest your thoughts, and others will perceive your vulnerability. They will treat you as someone who does not deserve respect and can be pushed around. Replace those old insecurities and fears with new empowering thoughts and reclaim your self-worth and self-esteem so that you can realize the success you deserve.

Learning to accept and re-affirm your true powerful position in life and remold your thinking will end your self-sabotaging behavioral patterns. New, empowering thoughts will yield the benefit of knowing that life has equipped you with everything you need to succeed.

Stop looking into the rearview mirror of your life and leave your hurts and insecurities behind. Look straight ahead with your head held high and get excited about your goals and where you want to go so that life can affirm all that you were born to be and do.

Early in life, you started to believe that you had some deficiencies, to the point where you believed them and tried to hide your true self for fear of being ridiculed or rejected. When you fear looking at your true self, you will find many ways to distract yourself from it. Sometimes, this could lead to addictions or other unacceptable behavior. However, in order to find your identity and accept who you are, you must stop running away from yourself and accept who you were born to be. Get to know the real *You* and start living the life you dreamed. When you stop running away from yourself, you'll reclaim a sense of peace and control over your life. Practice self-awareness and accept yourself as you are.

The acceptance you receive or don't receive from others reflects your self-acceptance. But don't confuse the two. When you accept yourself for who you are, the world will accept you. If you feel sad or frustrated because you don't feel respected, accepted, appreciated, or acknowledged by those around you, it is really a reflection of your own feelings.

When you embrace and accept yourself, the world will also accept you. You do not have to force or manipulate others to love, accept, respect, and honor you. Your self-respecting and accepting attitude will proceed from within you, and you will focus less on what others think. You will eventually drift away from those that do not match your opinion of yourself and grow closer to those that match and honor your inner guidance.

Life is about soaring beyond the limitations placed on you by society, family, even yourselves, so that when you come to the end of your life's journey, you will have no regrets about all of those things you wish you had done.

*"Be a first-rate version of yourself,
not a second-rate version of someone else."*
Judy Garland

CHAPTER 24
TRUST YOUR INNER GUIDANCE

"Trusting your intuition means tuning in as deeply as you can to the energy you feel, following that energy moment to moment, trusting that it will lead you where you want to go and bring you everything you desire."
Shakti Gawain

I am about to introduce you to an extremely powerful person. This person will be your travel partner providing all the guidance and tools you need along the journey of your career. This person is your *inner self*.

Only you can access what is inside of you, bring it forward, and make it a reality. Your inner self can visualize and realize an amazing career, because your true potential far exceeds what you have tapped into thus far. You can draw that full potential forward by focusing on your strengths and abilities.

Life is about free will, options, and choices; and no one but you can determine the ultimate path of your career. Your accomplishments and the realization of your dreams are up to you, because you can be all that your inner self has in store for you.

Intellectual knowledge can help you up to a certain point by providing information that will help you evaluate different options. However, when your decisions don't align with your inner guidance, you get that nagging voice second-guessing your decisions and motives.

As you assess your alternatives, you will look to various independent sources for guidance: your spouse, friends, family, co-workers, mentors—and even your boss. However, because of their differing backgrounds and life experiences, the advice you receive from each may conflict and be confusing to you as you strive to make informed career decisions.

Listen to all the well-intentioned advice and gauge it with your intuition, your gut feelings. When it is right for you, it will ring true in your heart and your gut. Take what works for you and leave the rest behind. Learn to trust your inner self—your inner compass—to help you build a solid foundation for a rewarding career, to help you move through significant transitions and barriers, and to point you toward your next step, the path that will lead you to that next plateau.

As you navigate your career, trust your intuition and gut feelings, and let your inner compass guide you along the way.

There will be no signs pointing out directions or written or unwritten rules to ensure your success. To achieve your greatest aspirations, exhibit the courage to take risks and explore unchartered territory, which may mean facing difficult situations that may end in failure.

Failure is not an accident

In life, nothing happens by accident or coincidence, and every experience is merely a steppingstone on the road to that next stage in your career. Failure results from actions, inactions, and reactions to your environment or situation. If you encounter failure, stop blaming others and look to the one place where limitations and insecurities breed and transcended: *in your own mind*. Failure has a definite purpose, structure, and sequence that gets your attention so you can make changes that will open new doors for you and take you to greater heights in your life and career.

Throughout your career there will be challenges and tough times. But it is imperative that you choose to regard these as opportunities and not roadblocks. Even though you may not understand the why or the how, embrace the challenges you encounter and view them as learning opportunities. If nothing else, you can learn something from a difficult situation, something that you can use to help you at a later stage. More often than not, some of these challenges turn out to be blessings in disguise.

Victim mentality

Take the time to understand the lesson that life has just delivered via the perceived failure so that you can make a plan and take definitive action to structure your next move. By asking what you can learn from an unpleasant situation, you have changed your mindset. When you change your attitude, you stop focusing on being the victim and instead take control by choosing to make the adverse situation part of your informal education. The stumbling block becomes the stepping-stone that will position you for that next career opportunity.

It will be extremely difficult for you to move forward with your career goals as long as you fixate on a victim mentality. Unfortunate events are a fact of life and need to be separated from your personal self-worth. It's not what happens to you, but how you react to what happens to you that sets your life in motion. As you grow and mature in your career, you will make good decisions that will propel you to new heights. Other times you'll make poor decisions that may cost you a career move. Your response to life's unfortunate events will determine how smooth or rocky your journey will be, and how many of those plateaus you can reach.

Wholeheartedly master your current assignment, so that experience can lead you to the next plateau of your career. Every goal, milestone, or change is accomplished one action at a time. So, continue along your path toward the realization of your goals, remembering that every road is traveled one step at a time.

Continue to believe in yourself

As you continue to travel patiently down your chosen path, the road may seem long, winding, and never-ending, and realizing your dreams may seem daunting, overwhelming, and, elusive. It may be difficult to remain optimistic when you see no evidence of your dreams coming to fruition. Continue to believe in yourself regardless of negative circumstances and input from those around you.

Your dreams may require time, energy, and other action on your part before they materialize. Stay positive, be optimistic, and keep plugging away at your major goals. Chances are you are doing much better than you think, and success is most likely just around the corner.

Do not let your boss, your coworkers, or your parents' or siblings' negative programming make you lose your self-esteem or self-worth. Your career should be about expanding your horizons and surfing on the cutting edge of your industry and environment. Amid your career, you may arrive at plateaus where you will rest, slowing down and taking it easy as you celebrate your accomplishments and success, but the time will come when you will be ready to move on and do more. For every milestone you reach in your career, there is always that next level beyond it that will take you to even greater career satisfaction.

> *"Life is the sum of your choices."*
> **Albert Camus**

CHAPTER 25

DEFINING CAREER SUCCESS

"Success is a self-fulling prophecy."
H. H. Swami Tejomayananda

Some of you are just embarking on your careers, others are in the midst of your mid-career, while some of you are counting down the days on the calendar towards retirement. But all of you have one thing in common. You all have a definition, or an idea of what career success looks like.

So, what does career success look like? How do you know if your career is successful? Is it becoming CEO, making it to middle or senior management, reaching a certain income level, getting a promotion every year or two, or getting that corner office? If you define career success by your job title, your position within the organization, or where you wind up at the end of your career, then you are missing the essence of your career experience.

Very few people will reach the heights of a Sonia Sotomayor, become President of the U.S., or become CEO of a Fortune 500 corporation. So, given those facts, does that mean that the rest of us were unsuccessful in our careers? Absolutely not!

Your career is a journey, not a destination. Along that journey you will encounter many conditions. There will be times when there is no congestion, no accident, traffic is light, and everything falls into place. Other times you will travel along a rocky road with many bumps, potholes, twists, and turns. A road that seems to be never-ending as one incident after other causes you stress and delay. You may also come upon a dead end, feeling stuck in a rut that seems impossible to overcome. Or, you may get caught up in a never-ending loop, where no matter what you do—right or wrong—you seem to go nowhere but back where you started.

Your career is not defined by where you end up as it is not a destination. Your career is a *journey* that is assessed by your integrity, how you traveled that road, the stops you made along the way, the people you met and inspired to reach their full potential, and the lessons you learned. Those lessons brought you full circle, making you not only the person you are today but also the one you will grow into tomorrow.

Your choices, actions, reactions, and inactions define the journey of your career in light of the opportunities and challenges life presents to you. You can have a rewarding career. Do not allow yourself to fail by false guilt, false criticism, and low self-esteem, or someone else's definition of success. Let your true essence magnify your highest capabilities and potential so that you can flourish in a rewarding and successful career so you can then proudly reflect on your career accomplishments.

Sometimes, you can achieve career satisfaction by mentoring others—in giving back. Take the time to invest in someone else. All it takes is a few minutes of your time to help others navigate their careers. I encourage you to take the time to give back, to "pay it forward," and to make a positive difference in the life of someone who can learn from your experience. It will amaze you at how it will positively affect your life and your career. Sometimes the definition of success is having reached back to help others achieve their full potential and career goals.

Defining your career is not about the company you work for, your job title, your salary or other perks. At its core your career success is about your self-evaluation, your sense of accomplishment, and your ability to define success for yourself, rather than letting others define it for you.

When planning the journey of your career, don't settle for a good or even great career; make *exceptional* your benchmark. Your career is a journey; so why not make it an *amazing* journey worth taking?

"Define success on your own terms, achieve it by your own rules, and build a life you're proud to live."
Anne Sweeney

BIBLIOGRAPHY

Fiction - Novel

Camila and Nic seemed to have it all—a loving marriage, two beautiful children, a cozy home, and a promising future. But beneath the surface, their perfect life was beginning to crack. Feeling neglected and unfulfilled, Camila embarks on a secret affair that threatens to unravel their world. As the truth comes to light, Nic is blindsided by the betrayal, left grappling with the disintegration of the life he once knew.

Self-Help / Spiritual

"Your Power Within—Inner Guidance" is a journey of self-discovery and healing. Through personal anecdotes and reflections, the book explores the quest for purpose and inner strength. It encourages readers to tap into their inner power, break free from limits, and create their dream life. This guide helps readers discover their passions, connect with their inner selves, and align with their greater purpose. Your inner power is limitless!

Memoir / Autobiography

What would you give up today for a better tomorrow? This question fuels an inspiring cross-generational journey from Spain to the US, spanning over 100 years. Through the characters' stories, we see the challenges and opportunities of immigration, acculturation, coming of age, and self-discovery. De La Rosa's transition from New York City's projects to corporate America highlights her personal and professional growth.

Self-Help / Career

A holistic approach is essential for upward mobility. Develop a career plan with clear goals and a forward-looking perspective.

Empower Yourself provides uplifting and inspiring insights. with practical advice and inner wisdom for workplace success.

REFERENCES

The "Vision Thing" Critical to Accelerating Women's Careers, By Suzanne Bates; Career Promotion Work Bloom; February 27, 2009.

"Why there are Differences in Gender Behavior" http://ebiz.netopia.com/learntolead/whyaretheredifferencesingenderbehavior/

Getting Beyond Career Failure; By: Victoria L. Rayner; Posted: June 26, 2008, from the July 2008 issue of Skin Inc. Magazine; http://www.skininc.com/spabusiness/management/ personnel/21804394.html

"Mothers hone leadership skills on career breaks", By Robin Gerber; USAToday.com, January 8, 2003

Albert, Camus. "Life Is a Sum of All Your Choices." – Albert Camus | Quotes | Dictionary of Quotes." *Quotes: Dictionary of Quotes*. Web. 15 Aug. 2011. <http://www.dictionary-quotes.com/life-is-a-sum-of-all-your-choices-albert-camus/>.

Burg, Bob. *Finestquotes.com*. Web. <http://www.finestquotes.com/author_quotes-author-Bob%20Burg-page-0.htm>.

Cloud, Glenda. *Quoteworld.org*. Web. <http://quoteworld.org/quotes/2940>.

Confucius. *Brainyquote.com*. Web. <http://www.brainyquote.com/quotes/quotes/c/confucius101164.html>.

How Can Disintegration be Positive? By Jesse Mannisto June 29, 2018; https://www.thirdfactor.org/how-can-disintegration-be-positive/

Drucker, Peter. *Finestquotes.com*. Web. <http://www.finestquotes.com/author_quotes-author-Peter%20Drucker-page-0.htm>.

Edison, Thomas A. *Buzzle.com*. Web. <http://www.buzzle.com/articles/short-inspirational-quotes.html>.

Fahmy, Miral. Reuters.com. Web. <http://www.reuters.com/article/2008/08/20/us-women-careers-idINSP29843720080820>.

Reuters printed the findings in an article entitled "Career women are their own worst enemies: study".

Freud, Sigmund. *Goodreads.com*. Web. <http://www.goodreads.com/quotes/show/94440>.

Goldsmith, Oliver. *Brainyquote.com*. Web. <http://www.brainyquote.com/quotes/quotes/o/olivergold121314.html>.

Green, Dennis. *Dictionary Quotes*. Web. <http://www.dictionary-quotes.com/the-secret-to-success-is-to-start-fromscratch-and-keep-on-scratching-dennis-green/>.

Larsen, Christian D. *Beliefnet.com*. Web. <http://www.beliefnet.com/Quotes/Inspiration/C/Christian-Larson/Believe-in-yourself.aspx>.

Olatunji, Babatunde. *Brainyquote.com*. Web. <http://www.brainyquote.com/quotes/authors/b/babatunde_olatunji.html>.

Rohn, Jim. *Personaldevelopmenttraining.com*. Web. <http://www.personal-development-training.com/2010/02/jim-rohnquotes.html>.

Roosevelt, Eleanor. *Quotationbooks.com*. Web. <http://quotationsbook.com/quote/20848/>.

Roosevelt, Eleanor. *Self-improvementmentor.com*. Web. <http://www.self-improvement-mentor.com/famous-leadership-quotes.html>.

https://keydifferences.com/difference-between-hearing-and-listening.html#:~:text=Someone%20rightly%20said%2C%20%E2%80%9CHearing%20is%20through%20ears%2C%20but,ears.%20It%20is%20the%20power%20 of%20perceiving%20sounds.

https://silo.pub/understanding-human-communication.html

Inspirational mentoring: Mentorship that matters | Together Mentoring Software (togetherplatform.com)

ABOUT THE AUTHOR

Blanca De La Rosa was born in the Dominican Republic. She grew up in the Projects of the upper west side of Manhattan in New York, during the time before the Hispanic population developed the supportive Latino community which exists today. Although she struggled without support in her cultural and linguistic transition, De La Rosa was able to graduate from Pace University with a Bachelor's Degree in International Business Management and to establish a successful 34-year career rising through the ranks of Mobil/ExxonMobil Oil Corporation.

During her career, she held numerous positions both domestic and international in nature with increasing responsibility. These assignments took her around the United States, Europe, Central / South America, and Nigeria.

De La Rosa retired from ExxonMobil after 34 years of service. As a Business Development Manager and President of the company's Employee Resource Group she often represented her company as lead presenter at the Regional and National Scholarship Awards hosted by the Hispanic Heritage Foundation. In addition, she represented her company as host, keynote speaker, and panelist of various events with organizations supported by the company's charity foundation. After all her time in the industry, she says her most rewarding role was serving as mentor to the young employees in her company – guiding them through the corporate maze.

I've often wondered what my life would have been like if we had not immigrated to the United States. When I visit this beautiful yet impoverished island of the Dominican Republic and see the need and want in the eyes of some of the people, I think, "That could have been me." So, I feel incredibly blessed and grateful for everything that I have been able to obtain and accomplish.

www.ingramcontent.com/pod-product-compliance
Lightning Source LLC
Chambersburg PA
CBHW030038100526
44590CB00011B/254